6

# The Anthropological Imagination in Latin American Literature

The

# Anthropological Imagination in Latin American Literature

## AMY FASS EMERY

UNIVERSITY OF MISSOURI PRESS
COLUMBIA AND LONDON

Copyright © 1996 by
The Curators of the University of Missouri
University of Missouri Press, Columbia, Missouri 65201
Printed and bound in the United States of America
All rights reserved
5  4  3  2  1     00  99  98  97  96

Library of Congress Cataloging-in-Publication Data

Emery, Amy Fass, 1957–
    The anthropological imagination in Latin American literature / Amy
Fass Emery.
        p.   cm.
    Includes bibliographical references and index.
    ISBN 0-8262-1080-5 (alk. paper)
    1. Latin American literature—20th century—History and criticism.
2. Literature and anthropology—Latin America.   I. Title.
PG7081.E64   1996
860.9'98—dc20                                    96-27401
                                                     CIP

 ∞™ This paper meets the requirements of the
American National Standard for Permanence of Paper
for Printed Library Materials, Z39.48, 1984.

Designer: Mindy Shouse
Typesetter: BOOKCOMP
Printer and binder: Thomson-Shore, Inc.
Typefaces: Garamond & Arial

To my parents,
Eli Norman and
Constance Converse Fass

# Contents

# ACKNOWLEDGMENTS

I would like to thank Jean Franco for being an incisive and always interested reader of this work when it was becoming a dissertation, and for valuable suggestions that aided its metamorphosis into a book. I am grateful to Diane Marting for bringing Clarice Lispector's short story "A menor mulher do mundo" to my attention, and for useful comments.

Ted Emery has been supportive of this project and its author in countless ways, and I would like to thank him with all my heart.

An early, shorter version of chapter 2 was published in *Hispanic Journal* and is reprinted here with the editor's permission. All unattributed translations are my own.

# The Anthropological Imagination in Latin American Literature

# THE
# ANTHROPOLOGICAL
# IMAGINATION

The conjunction of anthropology and literature in twentieth-century Latin American literary texts—what I am calling the "anthropological imagination"—is a wide-ranging phenomenon that encompasses the surrealist primitivism, *negrismo,* and *indigenismo* of the first half of the century, the prolific testimonial genre that began in the 1960s, and the "popular culture modernism" of the transcultural novel as theorized by Angel Rama. Major Latin American writers who can be said to share a specifically anthropological focus are many, and include Miguel Angel Asturias, Alejo Carpentier, José María Arguedas, Carlos Fuentes, and Augusto Roa Bastos.

Interest in anthropology's relation to literature and vice versa has emerged in recent years, following the poststructuralist challenge to science that has made both anthropologists and literary critics conscious of the rhetorical strategies they share. Historians and discourse analysts have pointed out that supposedly objective scientific discourses such as history and anthropology deploy plot structures and narrative devices that are subject to analysis in the same way as those of any literary text. At the same time, the postmodern critique of master narratives and universalizing systems finds in anthropology, whose focus is on the marginal, the local, the Other of totalizing Western paradigms, a discipline at the heart of postmodern sensibility.

The anthropological imagination has been fundamental in the ongoing process of defining Latin America's identity since Columbus arrived in the

New World and found it already inhabited. But while the first writings about an Other in Latin America begin simultaneously with the Conquest itself, interrelations between literature and the formalized discipline of anthropology emerge in the late nineteenth and early twentieth centuries, when anthropology acquired institutional status as a science.

Roberto González Echevarría has recently signaled the importance of anthropology for twentieth-century Latin American writers as "a set of given discursive possibilities . . . within and against which much of Latin American narrative is written."[1] However, González Echevarría's discussion of the development of the novel in relation to nonliterary discourses (in the colonial period to the discourse of law, in the nineteenth century to that of science, in the twentieth to that of anthropology) avoids any mention of specific schools of thought or paradigms of anthropology.

In this study I will look at how the exposure of twentieth-century Latin American writers to the discipline of anthropology and the various rhetorical styles and strategies specific to its various schools (cultural anthropology, functionalism, ethnography, etc.) is inscribed and recoded in their texts. An important consideration will be the extent to which Latin American writers conform to, and diverge from, metropolitan paradigms. I will also examine how changing images of the Other are reflected in anthropology and literature, and finally, I will discuss how the current disciplinary crisis in anthropology reverberates or is prefigured in Latin American writing, as well as anthropology's relevance to the vexed question of a Latin American postmodernism.

In general, my focus for this study has been the novel, for it is in the open-ended space of the twentieth-century experimental novel where inherited anthropological and literary conventions have been explored, questioned, and problematized, and where the objectivity demanded of the social scientist clashes with the more subjective and unstable border between Self and Other that characterizes Latin America's intercultural relations. My study does not propose to be an exhaustive survey, but rather focuses on representative writers and texts. As a result, some relevant writers have been necessarily excluded or relegated to the margins; notably, Asturias, Fuentes, and Roa Bastos.

In some cases, the writers I have chosen to include in this study— Alejo Carpentier, José María Arguedas, Miguel Barnet, Gregorio Martínez,

---

1. Roberto González Echevarría, *Myth and Archive: A Theory of Latin American Narrative*, 155.

Darcy Ribeiro, and Juan José Saer—have been both anthropologists and authors of fictional texts: this is the case with the Peruvian Arguedas and the Brazilian Ribeiro. Although he has written only literary, not scientific, texts, Barnet was trained as an ethnologist at the *Academia de Ciencias de Cuba*. Carpentier's anthropological imagination developed during his years in Paris, when avant-garde writers were closely allied with ethnographers (and sometimes also *were* ethnographers, as in the case of Michel Leiris, or wrote in an ethnographic mode, as did Georges Bataille). While neither the Argentine writer Saer nor the Peruvian Martínez have studied anthropology or frequented anthropological circles, the use they make of anthropological paradigms in their novels makes them relevant to my discussion here.

Although later chapters will be concerned primarily with the twentieth century, the "anthropological imagination" can be seen in a broader historical context. The study of native cultures in the sixteenth century was inspired by the needs of colonization—knowledge of the Other was required to enslave and deculturize—as well as by missionary zeal and a certain fascination with the Other's irreducible difference. The natives' cultural and religious practices were recorded and their oral "texts" translated in order to document idolatry and justify the coercive practice of conversion.[2] The incipient ethnographic tradition begun by friars and explorers was continued by European travelers to the New World like Jean de Léry, who found a moral lesson for the West in the Tupinamba of Brazil; even while describing Tupinamba cannibalistic practices, Léry contends that savagery was more in evidence in the Old World's spirit of intolerance that led to the rabid persecution of Protestants than in the gentle albeit cannibalistic Tupinamba.[3] The relative tolerance expressed by Léry and echoed in Montaigne did not characterize Enlightenment thinkers who, seeking to impose universal, totalizing strictures on local knowledge, called for the eradication of the superstitious, unenlightened practices of ignorant natives. What was seen as the work of the devil in sixteenth-century accounts was condemned as irrational barbarism from the Enlightened perspective of the eighteenth century and from the perspective of nineteenth-century positivism as well. The beginnings of modern anthropology in Latin America are tied to the racialist, ethnocentric assumption of evolutionary development from

2. For a critique and a history of anthropology as complicitous with the process of conquest and colonization from the fifteenth century to the present, see Jürgen Golte, "Latin America: The Anthropology of Conquest."

3. Jean de Léry, *History of a Voyage to the Land of Brasil*.

primitive to civilized societies formulated by Edward Tylor and Lewis Morgan in the nineteenth century, which remained influential as a paradigm well into the twentieth.

After World War I, the attitudes of Europeans toward their racial, cultural, colonized Other began to shift as they became aware of their own culture's potential for barbarity. The war eclipsed faith in the forward-moving thrust of unstoppable progress and eroded the self-assurance that they were on the right path. There was a sense that the colonized Other was in possession of something the West had lost: innocence, authenticity, natural rhythms, ties to the earth, a religious sensibility, and the stability of collective traditions in the face of, and as an alternative to, a chaotic, sterile modernity. In the twentieth century, the stigmatized Other of Western Christianity and Enlightenment becomes the alluring Other of Western Rationalism. The rise of ethnography is a symptom of, in Oswald Spengler's dramatic formulation, "the decline of the West."

## I. Ethnography and Surrealism versus Institutional Anthropology

James Clifford has identified ethnography in Paris in the 1920s and 1930s as a transgressive attitude about culture very much akin in spirit and practice to the avant-garde. Ethnographers and surrealists went in search of other traditions and their artifacts, which they opposed and juxtaposed as collage to those of the West in journals, museums, and expositions. Clifford calls this collaboration between surrealists and ethnographers "ethnographic surrealism."[4]

In their critique of Western civilization, and in support of their fascination for "primitive" societies as a counterpoint to the West, ethnographic surrealists drew on the theories of the French ethnologists Emile Durkheim and Lucien Lévy-Bruhl. For both, the primitive lived in a world marked by collective participation, in contrast to the "isolating, overdeveloped individualism" of modern civilization. Durkheim finds social harmony in primitive societies, while alienation and conflict characterize Westerners' social relations. Lévy-Bruhl's primitives think in a more mystical, less rational way than moderns because they are not conscious of the separation of world and self that underlies Western rationalism. For Durkheim, primitives have a religious faith that the West lacks, and that they demonstrate in ritual

---

4. James Clifford, "On Ethnographic Surrealism," in *The Predicament of Culture: Twentieth-Century Ethnography, Literature, and Arts,* 117–51.

acts that transcend individual isolation and confirm their ties to the sacred. The ability of primitives to project themselves onto a higher plane where they were in touch with cosmic forces, with an Other, more primal reality, attracted the surrealists in their desire to experience this more profound real (the sacred) that loomed beyond the world of appearances (the profane). The surrealists were also drawn to Freud's revelations of the unconscious, irrational forces in the mind that spoke of an Other world beyond the rational. In the unconscious (for Freud) and in the primitive (for Durkheim), "modern man would discover his own true nature, undisguised by the trappings of civilization."[5]

Surrealists and ethnographers, in escaping the spiritual poverty of the West, traveled in search of the alternative metaphysics of tribal and other "primitive" peoples. Ethnographic expeditions such as the 1931 Dakar-Djibouti expedition to Africa had their counterpart in the surrealists' pilgrimages to non-Western countries where they found the traditions of indigenous peoples were still more or less alive. They were especially drawn to the southern latitudes of the American continent—to Brazil, Haiti, and in particular to Mexico. Antonin Artaud arrived in Mexico in 1936, André Breton in 1938; Benjamin Péret was there from 1942 to 1947, while Pierre Mabille stayed from 1944 until 1946.

Despite the presence of surrealists and ethnographers such as Paul Rivet and Alfred Métraux, the ethnographic surrealism of the European avant-garde was out of sync with the social realities of post-Independence Latin America, and so it made little immediate impact on Latin American cultural life and literature. González Echevarría's vagueness with regard to anthropology leads him to apply Clifford's description of a collaborative effort engaging the combined forces of institutional anthropology and the avant-garde uncritically to Latin America, speaking broadly of "the convergence of avant-garde movements and the more widely accepted and institutional search for national identities."[6] But while it is true that institutional anthropology and the avant-garde traversed some common ground, the formulation that links the two phenomena together unproblematically in Latin America ignores that they had completely opposing aims, and were far apart ideologically.

5. Alice Letvin, *Sacrifice in the Surrealist Novel: The Impact of Early Theories of Primitive Religion on the Depiction of Violence in Modern Fiction,* 150, 15. My remarks about Durkheim and Lévy-Bruhl are based on Letvin's excellent discussion of surrealist primitivism.

6. González Echevarría, *Myth and Archive,* 154.

Surrealist travelers to America came with a priori, essentializing notions of "the primitive" that made them unable to take account of the actual social conditions they encountered. Luis Mario Schneider points out that when Artaud, disgusted with Western civilization, came to Mexico "to search for the roots of a magical culture that it is still possible to exhume from the native soil," the Mexican government was in the process of building a nation-state on the model of the same Western civilization from which the surrealists were anxious to escape.[7] Indeed, at the time when surrealists and ethnographers were imagining heterogeneity and cultural collage as challenges to the West, Latin American countries were attempting to forge national identities based on the acculturation or integration of their non-European Others—based on homogeneity. In most of the first half of the twentieth century, heterogeneity was seen by proponents of modernization in Latin America as a social problem, not, as for the surrealists, a means to escape from a dying, sterile civilization. The "decline of the West" was a literary conceit that ignored the actual, still vital, relations of power and domination between the West and its Others.

In *Del ayllu al imperio* (From Indian community to empire, 1925) the Peruvian *indigenista* Luis Valcárcel denounces heterogeneity as an obstacle preventing Peru from achieving a unified cultural identity. For Valcárcel, the mix of cultures resulted in "a new hybrid being": "The mix of cultures produces nothing but deformities." The rethinking of the role of indigenous populations in post-Independence Latin America produced an indigenism that was concerned with integrating those populations in the interest of nation-building. The seamless synthesis in which difference or hybridity is flattened out (and loses its potential for subverting hierarchies) seemed possible and advisable. José Vasconcelos's image of *mestizaje,* of a "cosmic race," is a universalizing, homogenizing one: "the fifth race . . . will fill the planet with the triumphs of the first truly universal, truly cosmic culture . . . the final race, the cosmic race." Theories that favor *mestizaje* thus envision an integrated whole in which indigenous populations are absorbed and disappear to create, in the words of the Mexican *indigenista* Andrés Molina Enríquez, "an authentic and powerful nationality that has a single life and a single soul."[8]

7. Luis Mario Schneider, *México y el surrealismo (1925–1950),* 61.

8. Valcárcel, Vasconcelos, and Molina Enríquez are cited in Manuel M. Marzal, *Historia de la antropología indigenista: México y Perú,* 466, 402, 403. My understanding of the development of anthropology in Latin America is indebted to Marzal's extremely valuable history.

Paradoxically, whereas surrealists found vitality and dynamism in non-Western traditions, the Indian as a social being in Latin America was perceived as immobile, resistant to the dynamic forces of modernization. In both Mexico and Peru, Indian cultures were compared to and described in terms of stone, in images of petrification. The anthropological study of native populations was undertaken in conjunction with American cultural anthropology's studies of acculturation, and not in the spirit of French ethnographic surrealism. If in the sixteenth century the native was studied with a view toward conversion, and in the eighteenth and nineteenth centuries in order to enlighten, in the twentieth century the study of Others in Latin America was undertaken in an effort to incorporate or integrate them into developing, modernizing nations; in the words of the Mexican anthropologist Manuel Gamio, Indian populations should be studied "with the exclusive objective of encouraging their development and incorporating them into contemporary civilization." For Alfonso Caso, founder of the Mexican *Instituto Nacional Indigenista* (1948), the purpose of indigenism was "the integration of indigenous communities into the economic, social and political life of the nation."[9]

The decline of the West as a crisis of conscience coincides with the institutionalization of anthropology as a discipline that paradoxically reaffirms the West's authority to collect, categorize—cannibalize—the Other's cultural capital as its own recedes. The two main currents in anthropology that had an impact on Latin America in the first half of the twentieth century were British social anthropology and American cultural anthropology. Social anthropologists studied the way in which individual societies functioned as organic units that could be studied in isolation by closely observing how the individual parts of a given society, in their interrelation, constituted a functioning whole. Cultural anthropologists studied individual cultures as isolable units as well, but they were also concerned with the phenomenon of diffusion, or the impact of external forces on a given culture's development. They undertook acculturation studies in order to document how traditional cultures responded to contact with modernizing forces.

An influential figure in American cultural anthropology as applied to Latin America was Robert Redfield, who developed a schema for studying the responses of rural, or what he called "folk," cultures to the process

9. Marzal, *Historia de la antropología indigenista,* 405, 411.

of urbanization.[10] Acculturation studies carried out in the 1920s through the 1940s presumed that modernization would prevail, that traditional societies despite their resistance to change would become acculturated and eventually disappear. After World War II, programs of applied anthropology in Latin America stressed development and modernization as goals for native populations. The Mexican anthropologist Ricardo Pozas participated in the *Instituto Nacional Indigenista*'s program of applied anthropology for the development of Indian communities in Chiapas. His *Juan Pérez Jolote* (1948), a novelized account of a tzotzil Indian's life, was influenced by Redfield's studies of folk versus urban mentalities. At the end of Juan Pérez's oddly inert monologue, it is clear that he is doomed to exactly reproduce the fatal slide of his father into alcoholism, smothered by the inability of his culture to respond creatively, or at all, to the forces of modernization.

In this context, it is not surprising that the ethnographic surrealism of the Parisian avant-garde was not immediately taken up by most Latin American writers. Mexican and Peruvian political indigenism had its literary counterpart in a novel that drew very much on traditional realist models. A few notable exceptions, however, pave the way for later developments: Alejo Carpentier's *¡Ecué-Yamba-O!* as an example of Caribbean *negrismo* (and Parisian *négritude*), and Mário de Andrade's *Macunaíma,* a product of the primitivism of Brazilian modernism. Significantly, the main revisionary stance of Brazilian modernism as articulated by Oswald de Andrade in his "Manifesto Antropófago" (1928) was a rejection of the passive acculturation model for Latin America in favor of a cannibalistic appropriation of European culture in order to forge an identity based on difference.

The technique of collage or juxtaposition cultivated by surrealists and ethnographers was not easily adapted to the novel as it was conceived in the 1920s and 1930s when *¡Ecué-Yamba-O!* (1933) and *Macunaíma* (1928) first appeared. Yet the inherently experimental nature of the novel— a genre in process without fixed generic constraints—made it the ideal, and perhaps the necessary space wherein the contradictions these writers faced and the ambivalence they experienced toward an Otherness at the heart of Latin America's problematic identity could be managed or worked through.

Both Carpentier and Andrade made use of a pastiche of heterogeneous sources culled from popular traditions that lent to their novels the form

---

10. Robert Redfield, *Tepoztlán, A Mexican Village: A Study of Folklife* (1930), and *The Folk Cultures of Yucatán* (1941).

and spirit of ethnographic surrealism. Carpentier draws on writings by ethnomusicologists, accounts of Afro-Cuban performances, photographs of Afro-Cuban instruments and artifacts, the writings of Fernando Ortiz on Afro-Cuban culture (as well as his documentary, ethnographic style), his own knowledge of Afro-Cuban speech patterns, the primitivism of Parisian *négritude,* the naturalism of the nineteenth-century novel, and assorted literary devices derived from the avant-garde. Andrade makes use of the German anthropologist Theodor Koch-Grünberg's collections of indigenous mythology, the rhythm of popular music, Afro-Brazilian ritual, and a pastiche of regional customs and vocabularies from all over Brazil.[11]

Predictably, these two difficult-to-classify novels perplexed contemporary readers: *Macunaíma* was not positively evaluated until the 1960s, while *¡Ecué-Yamba-O!* was never a success for its author. And, significantly, they both contained a fundamental ambivalence about the value of heterogeneity as a basis for establishing Latin American identity. In 1931, Carpentier stated that Latin Americans should embrace their difference from Europe, that they were defined by "the consciousness of being something other, of being something new, of being a symbiosis." At the same time, however, that *¡Ecué-Yamba-O!* presents the heterogeneity of Afro-Cuban culture as a dynamic process of synthesis that saves Cuba from being a copy of Europe, the residual influence of the early Ortiz's positivistic assessment of the black as a regressive, criminal element in Cuban culture cannot be ignored. Just as Carpentier's novel wavers between an emerging view of the Other as creative hybrid and a residual portrait of the Other as having a primitive mentality that is socially dangerous, Andrade's novel portrays a hero characterized by an indeterminate mixture of traits: at once dynamic and passive, heroic and cowardly, resolute and unable to resist temptation, neither Indian, nor black, nor white, he reflects the author's ambivalent attraction to and distaste for the Brazilian character as unstable, in process, the product of a heterogeneous mélange of inorganic elements.[12] Both authors want to value their difference from Europe, but their novels are

11. The novel's hero Macunaíma inherits his name and character from the cultural hero who is the protagonist of a series of myths collected in Koch-Grünberg's *Vom Roroima zum Orinoco II: Mythen und Legenden der Taulipang und Arekuná Indianern,* which Andrade used extensively as a source for his novel.

12. On the history of *Macunaíma*'s reception, see Silviano Santiago, "A trajetória de um livro"; Carpentier, *La novela latinoamericana en vísperas de un nuevo siglo,* 55; on Andrade's ambivalence, see Alfredo Bosi, "Situação de *Macunaíma.*" Roberto Da Matta discusses Macunaíma's unstable, inconsistent character in light of the folkloric tradition of

inconsistent in that they critique and celebrate Otherness at the same time. Dramatizing the ambivalence that difference represented for Latin American writers in the early years of the twentieth century, they straddle the line between nineteenth-century paradigms that stigmatize heterogeneity, and emerging paradigms that value the heterogeneous and the hybrid.

## II. Transculturation

Although the specific conjuncture of ethnography and surrealism produced few texts in Latin America, the avant-garde's critique of the West, its valorization of popular traditions and collective forms of life, and its subversion of hierarchies opened up the possibility of rethinking for the future the role of the Other in the constitution of Latin America's cultural identity. Brazilian primitivism's call for a cannibalistic ingestion and processing of the European inheritance, and Carpentier's perception of Latin America as "something new," "a symbiosis," prefigured the rejection of a passive acculturation leading to a homogenizing modernity as destiny as foreseen by cultural anthropologists.

In his influential *Transculturación narrativa en América Latina,* Angel Rama identifies a literary development in Latin America he calls "transculturation" (a term coined by Ortiz in 1940) that takes its impetus from the European avant-garde's critique of rationalism, but distances itself from the avant-garde in crucial ways. Like the surrealists, writers in the transcultural mode (Rama's list includes Juan Rulfo, Gabriel García Márquez, Augusto Roa Bastos, João Guimarães Rosa, and José María Arguedas) sought "a fertile contact with living origins."[13] They shared with surrealists the search for traditional, collective forms of life as a counterpoint to modern individualism, and found a sense of participation in the sacred in traditional societies that was lacking in Western culture. Unlike their predecessors, however, who invoked essentializing notions like "the primitive" or "le nègre," the transcultural novelists were steeped in the local context, and opposed specific local alternatives to the imposition of totalizing, universalizing Western paradigms.

According to Rama, the hierarchical distance the writer of a regional novel imposes between his own discourse and the local materials he

---

the *malandro* or *malandragem,* in *Carnivals, Rogues, and Heroes: An Interpretation of the Brazilian Dilemma*; see especially chapter 5.

13. Angel Rama, *Transculturación narrativa en América Latina,* 52.

represents in his text (language, practices, beliefs, etc.) is renounced by transcultural writers, who begin to write from within cultural practices that had been relegated to the status of objects of the civilizing gaze. Like the cannibalism of Brazilian modernism, transculturation is a process that involves responding to the imposition of European cultural and literary forms by transforming them according to the logic of local traditions in such a way as to create hybrid forms. Jorge Ibarra notes that for Ortiz, the concept of transculturation "implies that at the end of any process of reciprocal exchange between two cultures a new culture, different from the original ones, would emerge."[14] The recuperation and renewal of traditional forms of culture seen as a dynamic, contestatory process replaces the positivistic view of cultural development that envisions an evolutionary, uncontested drive toward progress and modernization based on the European model. As a result of this shift in focus from models of acculturation to models of transculturation, societies that had been seen as resisting modernity by being stubbornly inert, came to be seen as resisting by being creatively dynamic.

The creative resistance of Quechua culture to European domination becomes a utopian ideal in the work of the Peruvian writer and anthropologist José María Arguedas. Arguedas's "transcultural" imagination, however, derives from not literary but anthropological sources. The fundamental principle of the transcultural text as Rama explicates it is, it turns out, very close to the German American anthropologist Franz Boas's notion of "the genius of a people" that for each culture transforms influences from the outside according to its own idiosyncratic temperament or character. Boas's studies of folklore gave him a model for "the processes by which 'the genius of a people' acted to mold borrowed elements to a traditional pattern."[15] Arguedas's intensive studies of folklore in the 1950s, when the discipline was flourishing throughout Latin America largely through the impetus of Boas's example, led him to formulate a cultural poetics based on Boas's concept of the transcultural workings of "the genius of a people." Arguedas articulates the dynamic process involved in the creation of folklore, a process that becomes a model for his own narrative from the 1950s on, in a 1951 article entitled, simply, "Folklore": "Peruvian folklore is . . . eloquent proof of the vitality of Indian culture that has not been vanquished or

14. Jorge Ibarra, "La herencia científica de Fernando Ortiz," 1348.
15. George Stocking, "Introduction: The Basic Assumptions of Boasian Anthropology," 6.

arrested, as may be supposed, but rather assimilating constantly elements it has found necessary from Western culture, has transformed itself, creating the unstable and dynamic *mestizo*."[16]

Here the creative energy of Indian culture invents "a new culture, different from the originals," "a symbiosis." The same "vitality" that gives Indian culture its creative energy in Arguedas's formulation can be seen in Esteban Montejo, the protagonist of Miguel Barnet's 1966 *testimonio Biografía de un cimarrón* (*Biography of a Runaway Slave*). The Other in Barnet's book is a runaway black and a wanderer; eighteen years after Pozas's *Juan Pérez Jolote,* the Other acquires a kind of dynamism, in contrast to Pérez's inertia, inspired by the dynamic process of the Cuban Revolution and the same appreciation for the vitality of popular traditions that inspired the transcultural novelists. While native Indian groups had been stigmatized by stereotypes of their inertia, black populations were more easily associated with mobility and dynamism as the presence of blacks in the Americas was founded on a migratory experience, a historical situation that opens up the possibility for self-articulation as hybrid, situational, creative *bricolage*.[17]

In *Writing Culture: The Poetics and Politics of Ethnography* and *The Predicament of Culture: Twentieth-Century Ethnography, Literature, and Arts,* James Clifford discusses how the emergence of local, contestatory traditions has challenged the premises of anthropology as a discipline. According to Clifford, our contemporary, postcolonial world is made up not of the stable, self-enclosed premodern societies anthropologists once went to the field to encounter, but rather of cultures that interact globally, whose identities are "contested, temporal and emergent," products of "a hybrid, often discontinuous inventive process": "Everywhere individuals and groups improvise local performances from (re)collected pasts, drawing on foreign media, symbols, and languages." This contemporary "existence among fragments" has given rise to, in Clifford's view, an ethnographic, ironic approach to cultures in the ethnographic surrealist mode. The resurgence of an ethnographic perspective in the postmodern world follows "the disintegration of 'Man' as *telos* for an entire discipline": "To speak of 'man' and the 'human' is to run the risk of reducing contingent differences

16. José María Arguedas, *Señores e indios: acerca de la cultura quechua,* 173.

17. Michael Taussig puts the different symbolic constitution of the black and the Indian Other in these terms: "The black is cast as historical jetsam, matter out of place, the irrationality of history, while the Indian roots an order, an order of nature—as against history: matter in place." In *Mimesis and Alterity: A Particular History of the Senses,* 159.

to a system of universal essences." There can be no totalizing, essentializing discourses, for "[w]e are all Caribbeans now." In Clifford's utopian schema, "Caribbean" becomes a synonym for "a poetics of cultural invention," for the "hybrid and heteroglot," "polyphonic," "postcultural," "dis-orientation" that is our world. Today the West and its Others are all in the same fragmented boat, floating unanchored in a choppy Caribbean Sea.[18]

The situation Clifford describes might be perceived in some local settings in Latin America, but not others; he himself notes that the clash of indigenous populations with the forces of modernization has produced "results [that] have been both destructive and inventive." At the opposite pole of his own "metanarrative" of emergence and invention is "one of homogenization . . . of loss"; he admits that "[i]n most specific conjunctures both narratives are relevant, each undermining the other's claim to tell 'the whole story,' each denying to the other a privileged Hegelian vision."[19]

Renato Rosaldo has also cautioned that the celebration of heterogeneity and emergence is not the whole story: "the vision of the vanishing primitive has proven sometimes false and sometimes true. Confronted with the assaults of imperialism and capitalism, cultures can show remarkable resilience . . . and they can also disappear."[20] Arguedas's celebration of the "dynamic and unstable *mestizo*" as a figure of emergence was never the whole story for the writer, whose vision of Peru also included somber predictions for the future of areas where local traditions were weakened and disappearing, as in his lament for the loss of cultural traditions in "Puquio, a Culture in the Process of Change."[21]

From Arguedas's local standpoint, fragmentation can produce "irremediably well-developed individualisms" rather than a more desired collective inventiveness, "skeptical *mestizos*" in place of the "dynamic and unstable *mestizo*." At the same time that Arguedas was expressing optimism about an emerging mestizo identity, he was involved in the project of "salvage ethnography," collecting the folklore of Indian groups "before it was too late," and bitterly denouncing the indifference of the Peruvian government to the salvage of a "disappearing" indigenous patrimony.

18. James Clifford and George E. Marcus, eds., *Writing Culture: The Poetics and Politics of Ethnography*, 19; Clifford, *Predicament of Culture*, 10, 14; *Writing Culture*, 4; *Predicament of Culture*, 145, 173, 176.

19. Clifford, *Predicament of Culture*, 16–17.

20. Renato Rosaldo, *Culture and Truth: The Remaking of Social Analysis*, 81.

21. José María Arguedas, *Formación de una cultura nacional indoamericana*, 34–79.

Despite his announcement of the demise of essentializing anthropo-logical discourses, in his appropriation of "the Caribbean" as the model for a poetics of postmodern life in a world of fragments, Clifford in effect essentializes the black as a kind of wizard of invention, whose playful, synchretic behavior isn't all that far removed, one might feel, from images of the colonized as docile, dancing, premodern individuals. Significantly, Clifford does not locate synchretic, hybrid forms of resistance in the Amazon jungle, southern Chile, or Guatemala, where projects of national development have come into conflict with indigenous cultures, suppressing the emergence of local traditions. In his 1985 novel *Actas del Alto Bío Bío* (Recordings of the Upper Bio Bio River), Patricio Manns portrays the Mapuche Indians of Chile as an immobile, doomed race, stuck in the compulsion to repeat the same ineffective campaigns of resistance until at last they perish along with their names and their story. The elderly informants, whose taped dialogue with the journalist-narrator structures the novel, are "survivor victims" living in a region so remote from Clifford's intercultural synchretic utopia that they don't know what a tape recorder is. They live as if in slow motion, as if they were already dead, shielding themselves from the outside world. The old man, Angol Mamalcahuello, moves slowly and doesn't go far; the chief's wife, Anima Luz Boroa, wears a "funeral mask" for a face. The old man begins his dialogue with the narrator reluctantly, saying: "I no longer begin anything, mister. I'm now finishing with everything." When the narrator asks why they avoid the nearby towns and remain isolated, the old man responds that it was from that direction that the killers of his people came.[22] The contrast between Clifford's paradigm of emergence and this shell-shocked reaction to generations of genocide could not be starker. The narrator is incapable of forestalling the inevitable end; he has gone to interview the elderly Mapuche on a mission of salvage, to document their tragedy before they disappear. The anthropologist Anne Chapman brings "salvage ethnography" of this sort to its ultimate consequences in her *El fin de un mundo: los Selk'nam de Tierra del Fuego* (The end of a world: the Selk'nam of Tierra del Fuego, 1989), a collection of interviews with the handful of an ill-fated tribe who are its only survivors, in the last stages of their complete degradation.

22. Patricio Manns, *Actas del Alto Bío Bío,* 18–19, 13, 15.

### III. The *Testimonio*

The same effort to salvage through documentation a way of life that was disappearing produces the anthropological genre of testimonial narrative. The origins of *testimonio* in Latin America go as far back as the sixteenth century, when proto-ethnologists such as Bernardino de Sahagún created texts based on the "testimony" of native informants. The first modern examples of the testimonial genre were collections of the life histories of individual American Indians begun in the nineteenth century by anthropologists eager to popularize their craft, to make it accessible and alive for a broad audience. The subject of the American Indian evoked romantic, folkloric associations at a time when the unquestioned process of acculturation made the Indian past a source of nostalgia.

The life history in Latin America was prefigured by Robert Redfield's attempt to verify the existence of what he called a "primitive world view" through interviews with individual native informants.[23] The first actual life histories to be produced in Latin America were collected by Oscar Lewis, who was interested in the "culture" of poverty. Like the nineteenth- and twentieth-century anthropologists who published American Indian life histories, Lewis sought to make social science readable for the layman. He felt that the social sciences did not focus enough on the individual, and that the literariness of personal narrative had an appeal that would transcend the dryness of the scientific document.[24] Lewis's determination to merge art and science had a great influence on Miguel Barnet, whose *Biography of a Runaway Slave* started a prolific testimonial tradition in Latin America.

To some extent, the *testimonio* imitates the salvage ethnography of the American Indian life history in that its intent is necrological, to display as if in a museum relics from a distant, romanticized past: the *cimarrón* (runaway slave), the *pícaro,* the native. At the same time, however, the *testimonio* in Latin America has sought to represent the voice of emerging marginal populations, to recognize the Other as a social force rather than a social problem; thus it responds to the same revisionary impulse as the

23. Redfield explains the concept in his essay "The Primitive World View." See Calixta Guiteras Holmes, *Perils of the Soul: The World View of a Tzotzil Indian,* a work commissioned by Redfield, for an example of his methodology.

24. Susan M. Rigdon, *The Culture Facade: Art, Science, and Politics in the Work of Oscar Lewis.* Jean Franco also discusses Lewis in "Oedipus Modernized," *Plotting Women: Gender and Representation in Mexico,* 159–74.

transcultural novel. From the 1960s on, voices have emerged that contest official history, that counter the suppression of other, competing traditions, that transgress the imposition of silence.

The potentially revolutionary, counterhegemonic nature of *testimonio* has led some critics to contrast it to the postmodern trend that posits the radical disengagement of language from referentiality. George Yúdice has noted that while postmodernism and the testimonial genre apparently share a commitment to dismantling "master narratives" in order to give voice to the marginal realms of Otherness, against the *testimonio's* presentation of the voice of a flesh-and-blood other marginalized socially and politically from hegemonic sources of power, postmodernism constructs an Other as the locus of a metaphysical/aesthetic "sublime," an "absence," "the ineffable . . . that resides at the limits of language," a "generalized limit" which takes on the guise of woman, death, monster, savage, 'heart of darkness,' in sum, all that is abject."[25]

Like Yúdice, John Beverley is concerned to distinguish *testimonio* "as an extraliterary or even antiliterary form of discourse" from traditional literary models such as the novel. He contrasts the authenticity of testimonial discourse to novels that spuriously attempt to simulate a testimonial voice, and "fictionalizations of actual testimonial materials" or what he calls "pseudotestimonios."[26] Inherent in this argument for authenticity is the conviction that the literary somehow denatures or taints the real and trivializes the Other's struggle against oppressive social forces. While Yúdice recognizes that "testimonial writing is quite heterogeneous," his own criteria for authenticity privileges "those texts which are written as collaborative dialogues between activists engaged in a struggle and politically committed or empathic transcribers/editors."[27]

Yúdice and Beverley are suspicious of the tendency of certain literary critics to analyze the *testimonio* as a rhetorical construct. Beverley cautions against accepting Elzbieta Sklodowska's description of the problematic interplay of fiction and history in the *testimonio,* for "to simply subsume

25. George Yúdice, *"Testimonio* and Postmodernism," 22–23. While a distinction can and should be made between the "Other" as a discursive construct and the "other" as a flesh-and-blood human being, I have in general chosen to write "Other" with a capital "O" as my subject is anthropology and literature as discourses whose object is the rhetorically constructed cultural Other. The implications of writing the other as Other will be addressed throughout this study.

26. John Beverley, *Against Literature,* 84–85.

27. Yúdice, *"Testimonio* and Postmodernism," 17.

testimonio under the category of literary fictionality is to deprive it of its power to engage the reader . . . to make of it another (an-Other?) form of literature." Similarly, Yúdice faults literary critics like González Echevarría for having been "quick to discard the testimonialista's claim to authenticity, based on the age-old literary premise that narrative voice is always a persona which does not coincide with the individual narrating."[28]

For both Yúdice and Beverley, Miguel Barnet is an ambivalent figure. Beverley lists his *Canción de Rachel* (Rachel's song, 1970) as a text "located ambiguously between the authorial novel and testimonio," while Yúdice recognizes Barnet as "the most important writer and theorist of the testimonial in its early period" but in effect chastises him because "he continues to subscribe to the premises by means of which . . . institutions [educational, publishing, and professional] legitimize themselves."[29] Yúdice and Beverley's insistence on the nonliterary purity of the *testimonio* shrinks the parameters of the genre considerably, for not many narrative texts—as Hayden White and others have made clear—evade the effects of the literary. Indeed, even the definition of *testimonio* proffered by the revolutionary publisher *Casa de las Américas* in its contest rules soliciting outstanding contributions to the genre asserts that "literary quality is also indispensable." Although Beverley recognizes the "ambivalence" inscribed at the heart of the genre's conception, he is determined to argue "that a direct, 'unliterary' narrative might have both a higher ethical *and* a higher aesthetic status."[30] Significantly, the canonical pedestal achieved by Rigoberta Menchú's 1983 *testimonio Me llamo Rigoberta Menchú y así me nació la conciencia (I . . . Rigoberta Menchú: An Indian Woman in Guatemala)*, in both Yúdice's and Beverley's analyses (as well as in much critical writing on *testimonio*), highlights the singularity of Menchú's achievement and signals the dearth of comparably committed and readable works.[31]

Despite the genre's revisionary intent as eloquently argued by Yúdice and Beverley, critics of the *testimonio* have observed that its rhetoric reproduces the hierarchical relations of the larger society. Having the voice of the Other depend on the paternalistic presence of an interlocutor empowered to represent it signals the weakness of oral tradition, its dependence on

28. Beverley, *Against Literature,* 82; Yúdice, *"Testimonio* and Postmodernism," 18.

29. Beverley, *Against Literature,* 85; Yúdice, *"Testimonio* and Postmodernism," 19.

30. Beverley, *Against Literature,* 155.

31. See *Latin American Perspectives* 70 (summer 1991) for an example of the ubiquity of Menchú's text in considerations of the genre.

a writing that denatures it in order to preserve it. There is a potential for exploitation of the marginal Other as raw anthropological material to be processed for consumption, a reflection of economic exploitation of the Third World. Finally, unlike in Patricio Manns's novel, the tape recorder as mediator is banished from the scene of the *testimonio* in such a way as to simulate the spontaneity of oral speech and thus occlude the process by which the anthropologist-interlocutor intervenes in order to produce, rather than merely record and transcribe, the final text.

Less cautionary, others have seen in the inescapably double-voiced nature of the genre a contestatory space wherein the Other may make use of strategies of resistance to thwart the ethnographer/writer's illusory control over the text.[32] Nevertheless, such concerns regarding the representation of the Other's speech in *testimonio* can be seen as part of a similar debate going on in contemporary anthropology: how can the West portray Others without appropriating and objectifying them in a kind of discursive neocolonialism?

## IV. The Other Within

Traditionally, anthropological writings have repressed the subjective nature of the Self's encounter with the Other, in order to produce scientifically valid accounts of their objects of study. The necessary separation between Self and Other has perhaps always been especially problematic for writers and anthropologists in Latin America, where the distance between elite and popular classes has often not been absolute, has frequently been marked by cultural hybridity; in Néstor García Canclini's words, in Latin America "an inter-class *mestizaje* has generated hybrid formations in all social strata." In Latin America the Other coexists with the Self in a very real way, for the Self inhabits in many cases what Renato Rosaldo has called "the border zones" of culture, where identity is a matter of synchretic invention, of transculturation.[33]

According to Edward Said, "no identity can ever exist by itself and without an array of opposites, negatives, oppositions: Greeks always require barbarians, and Europeans Africans, Orientals, etc."[34] The ambivalence of

---

32. See for example Doris Sommer, "Rigoberta's Secrets."

33. Néstor García Canclini, *Culturas híbridas: Estrategias para entrar y salir de la modernidad,* 71–72; Rosaldo, *Culture and Truth,* 166.

34. Edward Said, *Culture and Imperialism,* 52.

this oppositional stance of the Self toward the Other in Latin America has been documented as far back as the sixteenth century, when friars like Bernardino de Sahagún spent endless hours diligently preserving in writing the same "savage" practices they were intent on destroying. The accounts of native life produced by friars and explorers betray a subliminal fascination for the Other whose difference they explicitly condemn. Similarly, it has become a commonplace to note that advocates of progress and enlightenment in the nineteenth century like Domingo Sarmiento were attracted to the vitality of the same idiosyncratic native practices they denounced as barbaric and recommended eliminating as soon as possible.

This ambivalent attraction of the civilizing forces toward the Other to be repressed is evident as well in classic twentieth-century Latin American novels such as William Henry Hudson's *Green Mansions* (1904), José Eustasio Rivera's *La vorágine* (The vortex, 1924) and Rómulo Gallegos's *Canaíma* (1941). In these novels, civilization in the guise of the hero-protagonists sets itself as a guiding light to be wielded against the regressive forces that rule the anarchic jungle and the lawless *llano,* but ends up giving in to, being seduced by, the dark savage barbarity that assaults the tenuous borders of the civilized Self. The startling intimation in these novels of a savage Other within the Self signals an erosion of faith in the embattled forces of civilization and prefigures, in Cornejo Polar's words, "the discovery that the Other resides in the most intimate cloister of the Self."[35]

Recent critics of anthropology have denounced the discipline's claim to speak from an objective, neutral stance. According to Renato Rosaldo, "once-dominant conceptions of truth and objectivity" have been "eroded" by a growing distrust of master narratives and totalizing sciences. In this contemporary, "postmodern" age there is the sense that truths can only be "partial," situational and local, and that anthropologists cannot transcend their own subjective judgments based on their limitations as "positioned subjects" who can only know what their specific situational positioning allows them to know. Latin American anthropologists are, in this sense, "positioned subjects" whose socially conditioned, intimate relation to the Other lends their writing, in Martin Lienhard's words, "a more immediate, more existential social significance."[36]

35. Antonio Cornejo Polar, "Las figuraciones transculturales en la obra de Augusto Roa Bastos," 10.
36. Rosaldo, *Culture and Truth,* 21, 8. Martin Lienhard, *La voz y su huella: escritura y conflicto étnico-social en América Latina,* 243.

The rejection of objectivity as a viable stance toward the Other can be seen in several writers whose works I discuss in this study: José María Arguedas, Darcy Ribeiro, and Miguel Barnet. Both Arguedas and Ribeiro have written authoritative anthropological texts, from a scientific, "objective" point of view, but they have also written texts where the line is not so clear between objective and subjective knowledge about cultural Others (critics have noted the lyrical aspect of many of Arguedas's anthropological essays; Ribeiro's *Fronteras indígenas de la civilización* contains several personal anecdotes) as well as texts that actually problematize objectivity and present alternative ways of knowing based on the Other's store of traditional knowledge (Arguedas's *Los ríos profundos* [*Deep Rivers*], Ribeiro's *Maíra*).

All three of these writers, trained as anthropologists, have written fables of intimacy that authorize them to speak of the Other not as detached social scientists, but as Selves intimately involved with the Others they represent. Arguedas draws on his childhood experience of intimacy with the Indian world; virtually raised by Quechua Indians, his story goes, he was steeped in a profoundly lived experience of native folklore, ritual, music, and daily life that his subsequent training as an anthropologist could not surpass. Arguedas opposed traditional knowledge to science: "folkloric knowledge can only be learned in a traditional context: by word of mouth, by oral explanation, by imitation" while "[f]olklore as a science can only be learned at universities and specialized institutes." Although Arguedas's scientific knowledge was vast, he consistently drew on the symbolic capital of his fable of intimacy as the source of his authority to speak of the Other: "only those who have listened since childhood to Indians speaking" can penetrate the richness of their speech, not the linguist. Just as the Indian narrator (or narrators) of *Dioses y hombres de Huarochirí* (Gods and men of Huarochirí, 1966) derives authority from his status "not as an observer but as a participant" according to Arguedas, he rejects for himself the position of outside observer, and promotes the myth of his authoritative, because authentic and unscientific, insider's view.[37]

Darcy Ribeiro looks back fondly on his ten years of fieldwork among Amazon Indian tribes in Brazil as "the best years of his life."[38] This nostalgia is based on the relation of intimacy that he established with the Kadiwéu.

37. José María Arguedas, "¿Qué es el folklore?"; *Canciones y cuentos del pueblo quechua*, 68; Francisco de Avila, *Dioses y hombres de Huarochirí*, 10.
38. Speaking of himself in the third person in *Sobre o obvio*, 9.

Ribeiro's subjective involvement led him to reject the objectification of the Other required in the functionalist studies he undertook as a young man, and some years later to write a novel in which the fragmenting of perspective represents a refusal of the authoritative, totalizing documentary realism of the functionalist monograph.

As with Arguedas and Ribeiro, Barnet's vocation as a scientist conflicts with his desire for intimacy and fusion with the Other. He notes that his formation as an ethnographer required him to use a methodology based on the principles of social science.[39] Nevertheless, in a more compelling version of the encounter between ethnographer and informant in *Biography of a Runaway Slave,* he explains how in the process of writing he suppresses the Self and becomes the Other: "I was the character . . . there comes a moment when you find you're in the hills talking with the trees . . . Do you understand? You are an Other." Although Barnet's science implicitly reproduces the relation of master (Barnet/anthropologist) to slave (Montejo/*cimarrón*), he explicitly rejects the hierarchical relation of the Self toward the Other by signaling his desire to reverse roles, to play slave to the Other as master, to "serve humbly as a resonator for the voice of others."[40]

## V. The Metaphysics of Otherness

Anthropology's self-questioning has led the discipline to a self-reflexive critique of itself as a discourse, and a relation to the Other that is discursive rather than existential in nature, in Lienhard's sense. Paul Rabinow has recently sounded a cautionary note with regard to the self-reflexive trend in anthropology that echoes Yúdice's critical comments on the postmodern construction of a disembodied Otherness: "The metareflections on the crisis of representation in ethnographic writing indicate a shift away from concentrating on relations with other cultures to a (nonthematized) concern with traditions of representation, and metatraditions of metarepresentations, in our culture." James Clifford, Rabinow suggests, "is not talking primarily about relations with the other, except as mediated through his central concern, discursive tropes and strategies."[41] In *Myth and Archive,*

---

39. In Edna Acosta-Belén and Jean-Philippe Abraham, "Encuentro con Miguel Barnet," 48.

40. Cited in Emilio Bejel, "Entrevista," 49; Acosta-Belén and Abraham, "Encuentro con Miguel Barnet," 48.

41. Paul Rabinow, "Representations Are Social Facts: Modernity and Post-Modernity in Anthropology," 251.

González Echevarría defines anthropology as "a scientific discourse whose object is not nature, but essentially language and myth"—in other words, a metadiscourse. Once he has defined anthropology in this way, it is not surprising to find that of the texts González Echevarría analyzes at length as he argues that anthropology is the primary mediating discourse of twentieth-century Latin American literature (Borges's "Tlön, Uqbar, Orbis Tertius," Carpentier's *The Lost Steps,* García Márquez's *One Hundred Years of Solitude,* and Barnet's *Biography of a Runaway Slave*), only Barnet's is directly concerned with an actual other, or that Columbus's contemporary fray Ramón Pané can become an honorary Borgesian *avant la lettre.*[42]

The disengagement of the Self/Other relation from its sociopolitical content in contemporary discourse reflects the location of Otherness in the inaccessible, intimate recesses of the Self as seen in poststructuralist thinkers like Michel Foucault, Jacques Lacan, and Michel de Certeau. In his 1983 novel *El entenado* (*The Witness*), Juan José Saer situates anthropological discourse in the context of poststructuralist thinking on the interrelations of subjectivity, Otherness, and language. Anthropology and literature are seen in Saer's novel as elegiac discourses structured by language's always-deferred desire to capture the inaccessible real. The anthropological imagination thus repeats in its longing for the inaccessible Other a structure of desire inherent in language itself.

The chapters that follow will return to the issues that have been introduced here in close textual analyses of individual works. Chapter 2 focuses on Carpentier's use of collage—an aesthetic device common to the surrealists and ethnographers the Cuban writer knew and with whom he collaborated during his years in Paris—as the model for a new, celebratory vision of Afro-Cuban culture as hybrid. In chapter 3 I will argue that Arguedas's frustrated desire for intimacy with the Other is resolved or exorcised on an imaginary level in compensatory fictions that assert the Self's hierarchical position of control over the elusive Other. This conflict between the desire to objectify and control the Other through the mastery of science and the desire to fuse with the Other is also evident in Barnet, whose *Biography of a Runaway Slave* I discuss in chapter 4. Both Arguedas and Barnet reveal in their works a fundamental ambivalence toward the will to power inscribed in ethnographic discourse. In chapter 5, I discuss how Ribeiro rejects the functionalist monograph's pretension to arrive at

42. González Echevarría, *Myth and Archive,* 13, 145.

an ultimate, totalizing truth about the cultural Others they document by writing a fragmented, modernist novel in which he portrays an Amazon Indian tribe as an impenetrable enigma. Finally, chapter 6 deals with Saer's *The Witness,* a novel the author sets in the sixteenth century at the originary moment of violent contact between the European Self and the native Other in order to suggest that anthropological writing reenacts on a symbolic level both the violence and the desire expressed in acts of conquest, colonization, and genocide. Saer's novel rewrites the conflict between the will to mastery and the desire for communion common to all the writers discussed in this study, as a metaphysical parable about the Self's imaginary conquests, betrayals, and fables of intimacy in the inaccessible, endlessly fantasized realm of the Other.

# 2

## THE "ANTHROPOLOGICAL FLÂNEUR" IN PARIS
*Documents, Bifur,* and Collage Culture in Carpentier's *¡Ecué-Yamba-O!*

The influence of surrealism on the Cuban writer Alejo Carpentier has been well documented. One aspect of Carpentier's surrealist connection that has not been studied, however, is his active involvement in the production of the influential Parisian journals *Documents* (1929–1930) and *Bifur* (1929–1931). Although he contributed only one article to *Documents* on Cuban music, Carpentier's name invariably appears among the list of collaborators that accompanied each volume of the journal. In *Bifur* his presence is also consistent; he contributed an article, a translation of an article by Ramón Gómez de la Serna, and participated in a panel discussion with Ribemont Dessaignes, Varèse, Huidobro, and others.[1] There is abundant evidence of Carpentier's close association with those involved in the production of these journals. His friendship with Robert Desnos is well known. He collaborated with Georges Ribemont Dessaignes, the editor of *Bifur* and a contributor to *Documents,* on a libretto for *The one alone* by Edgar Varèse.[2] He evokes his friendship with Georges Bataille, the editor of *Documents,* in a 1956 letter in which he reminisces about the journal—"a journal in which everything that came later had already been expressed . . . in almost prophetic fashion."[3]

1. Alejo Carpentier, "La musique cubaine," "Lettre des Antilles," "Le 'Cante Jondo,'" "La mécanisation de la musique."
2. Carpentier, "Edgar Varèse escribe para el teatro."
3. For the full text of the letter, see Carmen Vázquez, "El mundo maravilloso de Carpentier."

*Documents* and *Bifur* disseminated the contemporary vogue of surrealist primitivism, presenting in their pages interfaces of the tribal (the "primitive") and the modern. Articles on Picasso, Matisse, Masson, and de Chirico were juxtaposed to articles on primitive art and societies, glossy prints of surrealist paintings coincided with photographs of primitive art, and images of African tribal societies appeared together with icons of industrial development like skyscrapers or machines, or with images of contemporary Parisian cultural life like *clochards* (the homeless), scenes from films, or music-hall dancers. The technique of pastiche or "collage" in these journals reflected the surrealists' enthusiasm for unexpected juxtapositions as a means of altering conventional perceptions of reality. Ethnography, which emerged as a discipline in the 1920s, together with surrealist primitivism, challenged received ideas about Western civilization and its Others at a time when the dominance of Western culture as a discrete entity was profoundly in question for the post–World War I generation.[4]

Carpentier's exposure to what James Clifford has called the "ethnographic surrealism" of the Parisian avant-garde is evident in the articles he wrote for *Social* and *Carteles* during his years in Paris (1928–1939), in *¡Ecué-Yamba-O!* (1933), and beyond. I will focus specifically in this chapter on the use of the ethnographic gaze in his portrayal of Afro-Cuban culture, on his departure from Fernando Ortiz's positivistic anthropology, and on the use of surrealist collage to evoke the dissonant heterogeneity of Latin American reality—a crucial concept that anticipates his theory of the baroque as the fundamental style of Latin America. For European-born surrealists, the collage paradigm expressed their perception of a reality that was disintegrating—a reality that had seemed stable prior to the turn-of-the-century crisis that was diagnosed and aestheticized in the fragmented works of the Modernists.[5] For Carpentier, Latin American reality presented itself as already fragmented, already marked by a hybrid mixture of styles. Latin America's hybrid nature became a way for Carpentier to reinvent collage, embracing the avant-garde while at the same time distancing himself from Europe. Just as he recast the surrealist "merveilleux" as a "marvelous realism" indigenous to America, Carpentier

4. See James Clifford's discussion in *Predicament of Culture*, 117–48. The expression "anthropological *flâneur*" in my title is used by Clifford to describe Lévi-Strauss in New York City in the 1940s in his essay "On Collecting Art and Culture," 238.

5. For an account of this history, see Christopher Butler's *Early Modernism: Literature, Music, and Painting in Europe, 1900–1916*.

would find an autochthonous version of surrealist collage in Afro-Cuban synchretism.

The heterogeneity of sources and their presentation in *Documents* and *Bifur* as collage mirrored the "collecting" of cultural artifacts associated with ethnography. One purpose of ethnographic missions to Africa such as the Dakar-Djibouti expedition (whose participants were also contributors to *Documents*) was to "collect" the treasures of tribal villages and bring them back for display in Western museums and galleries. In fact, the spoils were labeled "booty" by those involved in the expedition.[6] Like ethnographers, the surrealists were collectors. They frequented flea markets in search of tribal and Western cultural artifacts that, decontextualized, spoke to them of Other, exotic worlds.

Carpentier confesses his own passion for collecting in "La Exposición Internacional de París." What strikes him at the Exposition is a display of folk art from Portugal, which evokes a similar collection on display in his own Paris studio:

> Mexican toys, Andalusian ceramics, animal-shaped bottles from Cuenca, earthenware from Badajoz, ex-votos of Lusitanian sailors, Afro-Cuban instruments, Javanese marionettes and Venezuelan ponchos acquired in my travels or given to me by friends . . . who know my *weaknesses*!

> (juguetes mexicanos, cerámicas andaluzas, botellones de Cuenca en forma de animales, barros de Badajoz, exvotos de marinos lusitanos, instrumentos musicales afrocubanos, marionetas javanesas y ponchos venezolanos, adquiridos por mí en distintos viajes, o regalados por amigos . . . que conocen mis *debilidades*!)[7]

Carpentier's "collecting" can be seen as parallel to ethnographic collecting, as both involve transferring the products of popular or "primitive" cultures from the periphery to the center (Paris). In both cases, the original context in which the objects have been produced and used within a particular cultural setting has been ignored as they become recontextualized aesthetic objects in a studio/museum. Collecting is a way to fetishize the products of the periphery and constitute the center as the space to which these products must be relinquished, and in which they are subjected to

6. Clifford, *Predicament of Culture*, 137.
7. Alejo Carpentier, *Obras completas* 9: 418.

the "nostalgiac cannibalism" of the West's controlling gaze.[8] In Carpentier's studio/museum, Javanese marionettes, Afro-Cuban instruments, and Venezuelan ponchos signify "the exotic" as collage for European eyes.

The display of cultural pastiche was the purpose of the *Exposition Coloniale* of 1931 in Paris, which celebrated the "successes" of French colonialism and which Carpentier bears witness to in his "Segundo viaje a la Exposición Colonial" (Second trip to the Colonial Exposition):

> Near an ornamental pond the blacks' bells and drums are heard; Chinese trumpets accompany battles of the gods at the Theater of the Far East; orchestras from the island of Bali invent counterpoint rhythms, that by a rare ethnic coincidence have the faint flavor of a criollo *son*; screechy violins and Moroccan *botijuelas* make an infernal racket in the Arab café. . . .

> (Cerca de un estanque, suenan cencerros y tambores negros; las trompetas chinas acompañan combates de dioses en el Teatro de Extremo Oriente; las orquestas de la isla Bali inventan contrapuntos de ritmos, que por rara coincidencia étnica tienen lejano sabor de *son* criollo; los violines chillones y las botijuelas marroquíes arman estruendo infernal en la café árabe. . . . )[9]

This description of the Colonial Exposition evokes the collagelike, incongruous juxtapositions cultivated by surrealists. The cultural pastiche in evidence at the Exposition bears a striking resemblance in turn to Carpentier's experience of cosmopolitan Paris; for everywhere the Cuban writer went he encountered exotic "spectacles of cosmopolitanism." He describes his activities as a *flâneur* in the streets of Paris exploring "a thousand hidden corners the tourists will never find."[10] In "El encanto cosmopolita del Barrio Latino" (The cosmopolitan charm of the Barrio Latino) he marvels at the cultural pastiche on view:

> There are ambassadors from Oxford sporting knickers and red ties; there are Russian and Scandinavian women with lively gazes and manly gaits. You see Indians from our America who hang out with the

8. Claude Lévi-Strauss uses the phrase "nostalgiac cannibalism" in *Tristes Tropiques*: "Not content with having eliminated savage life, . . . it [Western civilization] feels the need feverishly to appease the nostalgiac cannibalism of history with the shadows of those that history has already destroyed," 31.

9. Carpentier, *Obras completas* 8: 286.

10. Carpentier, *Obras completas* 8: 239, 224.

blondest women in the neighborhood; you see Egyptian doctors. . . .
The Chinese students from the Barrio Latino alone constitute a veritable
colony . . . In the area around the Sorbonne you could see a hundred
Hindu turbans, and even the brown silk tunics of Afghani university
students.

(Hay embajadores de Oxford, que lucen *knickerbockers* y corbatas
rojas; hay rusas y nórdicas, de viva mirada y andar varonil. Se ven
inditos de nuestra América, que se hacen acompañar por las mu-
jeres más rubias de todo el barrio; se ven doctores egipcios. . . . Los
estudiantes chinos del Barrio Latino constituyen, por sí solos, una
verdadera colonia . . . En los alrededores de la Sorbona podríais ver
cien turbantes hindúes, y hasta las túnicas de seda parda de bachilleres
afganos.)[11]

Carpentier here perceives the migration of the marginal to the center
(to Paris) as an incongruous, circuslike spectacle. The center has been
invaded by Indians in the company of blonde women, Afghanis who study
at the Sorbonne, and Chinese who have established an entire colony in
the Latin Quarter. The colony has arrived to reclaim its place at the center,
and its arrival creates an exotic, decentering heterogeneity represented as
collage.

The style of accumulation or juxtaposition that translates visual collage
into language—Carpentier's *flâneur's* eye view of Paris—recalls as well
that of Louis Aragon in *Le paysan de Paris*. Aragon's ethnographic eye
defamiliarizes Parisian culture and its artifacts as it focuses on the display
of objects in stores and store windows; in a traditional barbershop he lists:

toilet cases and flasks . . . linen gloves, pliable or unbreakable combs
. . . nail files and all the accoutrements that make mannicure a species
of white magic; cosmetics and fright philters; soaps of every description, green, pink and yellow soaps . . . toothbrushes and dentrifices;
salts for migraine headaches, and the vapors, eyewashes and miracle
creams.

(trousses et flacons . . . les mains de linge, les peignes pliants ou incass-
ables . . . les limes et tout ce qui fait du soin des mains une blanche
magie, et les fards, et les philtres d'éffarement; et les savons, verts,
roses, jaunes . . . et des brosses à dents, les dentifrices, les sels pour la
migraine et les vapeurs, les eaux pour les yeux, les pâtes à miracles.)[12]

11. Carpentier, *Obras completas* 8: 240.
12. Louis Aragon, *Nightwalker*, 76–77; *Le paysan de Paris,* 117.

This pasting together of a disparate collection of objects is a stylistic device that Carpentier adopts frequently in his journal articles, as in "Una visita a la Feria de las Pulgas" (A visit to the Flea Market):

> You see old, dirty books; stuffed animals, sad and dusty; paintings and sculptures of failed artists; ancient furniture with slashed cushions; a pelican hunted in the Niger, and a swan whose stuffing is coming out its side . . . false teeth and forceps; glass eyes that try to roll toward nearby telescopes; decapitated manniquins. . . .

> (Se ven libros viejos y sucios; animales embalsamados, polvorientos y tristes; pinturas y estatuas de artistas fracasados; muebles antiguos con cojines acuchillados; un pelícano cazado en el Níger, y un cisne mirando que llora miraguano por el costado . . . dentaduras postizas y fórceps; ojos de vidrio que tratan de rodar hacia catalejos cercanos; maniquíes decapitados. . . . )[13]

The perception of heterogeneous elements juxtaposed as collage is fundamental to Carpentier's portrayal of Cuban culture in *¡Ecué-Yamba-O!* While Carpentier turns an ethnographic eye on Paris in his writings for a Cuban audience published in *Social* and *Carteles*, conversely he adopts an ethnographic perspective with respect to Cuba for his European readers in *Documents, Bifur,* and *¡Ecué-Yamba-O!* Compare his description of the Exposition and the streets of Paris to this passage from the novel:

> The phonograph from the Chinese store ejaculates Cantonese songs of love. The fat bagpipes of some Gallegan argue with the asthmatic accordions of the Haitian. The bongo drum skins vibrate in sympathy, discovering Africa in the songs of the people of Kingston.

> (El fonógrafo de la tienda china eyacula canciones de amor cantonesas. Las gaitas adiposas de algún gallego discuten con los acordeones asmáticos del haitiano. Las pieles de los bongoes vibran por simpatía, descubriendo el Africa en los cantos de la gente de Kingston.)[14]

The same cultural pastiche that lends to Paris an exotic albeit incongruous cosmopolitan panache can be seen in Cuba where a counterinvasion—from the center to the periphery—is accomplished:

13. Carpentier, *Obras completas* 8: 235.
14. Alejo Carpentier, *¡Ecué-Yamba-O!*, 15. Subsequent page references to the novel will be made parenthetically in the text.

Mobs of workers. American foremen chewing tobacco. The French chemist . . . The inevitable wandering Jew . . . squadrons of raggedy Haitians emerging from the far-off horizon bringing their women and fighting cocks . . . Then Jamaicans with square jaws and discolored overalls arrived . . . Soon Gallegan emigrants appear . . . Some tenacious Poles improvise run-down shops. . . .

(Tropeles de obreros. Capataces americanos mascando tabaco. El químico francés . . . El inevitable viajante judío . . . escuadrones de haitianos harapientos, que surgían del horizonte lejano trayendo sus hembras y gallos de pelea . . . Después llegaban los de Jamaica, con mandíbulas cuadradas y *over-alls* descoloridos . . . Pronto aparecen los emigrantes gallegos. . . . Algunos polacos tenaces se improvisan tenduchos. . . . ) (12–13)

Whereas for surrealists like Aragon pastiche is a function of the surrealist imagination in search of chance juxtapositions of the incongruous, here pastiche translates the discordant colonial condition of Latin America as French chemists, American foremen, raggedy Haitians, Gallegan emigrants, and tenacious Poles come together in a chaos produced by the unnatural rhythm of a colonial economy.[15] The view of Cuba as a collage culture is reinforced by the inclusion of photographs of black fetishes and drawings of exotic Chinese customs in a style as reminiscent of *Documents* and *Bifur* as of Fernando Ortiz's *Hampa afro-cubana: los negros brujos* (Afro-cuban underworld: the black sorcerers, 1906).[16] Ortiz based his ethnographic studies of black culture in Cuba in part on fetishes of the black religion that were seized by police during raids on houses of those suspected of witchcraft (*brujería*). He makes this clear repeatedly and unself-consciously in his study, and even calls the seized objects "booty" (botín).[17] He incorporates the confessions or self-defenses of the accused blacks into his archive of knowledge, seemingly innocent of the relations of power that produce their testimony and his interpretations.

Ortiz includes in his text photographs of the fetishes seized by police and retained like ethnographic collections as evidence of criminal behavior. He

15. Kumkum Sangari makes the distinction between a surrealist aesthetics of surprise and a marvelous realism that in Latin America "embodies a *specific* social relation," where "the casting up of the strange, the incongruous, the peripheral, is the *product* of a historical situation." In "The Politics of the Possible," 160.

16. Roberto González Echevarría discusses the influence of Ortiz on the Afro-Cuban movement in general and on Carpentier in particular in *Alejo Carpentier: The Pilgrim at Home,* 34–96.

17. Fernando Ortiz, *Hampa afro-cubana: Los negros brujos,* 51.

in turn reproduces them as evidence of the "African fetishist" unchanged and unrepentant beneath the facade of Catholic conversion: "as soon as one scrapes off that outer layer of relative religious civilization one will uncover the African fetishist." Ortiz's display of photographs repeats textually the original violence of confiscation and recoding that takes place at the police station, while photographs of the accused sorcerers (*brujos*) included in *Afro-Cuban Underworld* similarly double as mug shots. Ortiz's rhetorical strategy is that of a detective uncovering evidence in order to bring the Other into the orbit of control of his anthropological discourse. The objects then become transposed to a Western economy that assigns them a value within that economy: "A sorcerer who had the misfortune of having his *jimaguas* fall into the hands of the authorities offered more than twenty *pesos* of gold for their return. In spite of this high esteem, they're nothing but crudely made wooden dolls . . ."[18]

In *¡Ecué-Yamba-O!* Carpentier collects and displays the *same kinds of photographs* we see in *Afro-Cuban Underworld,* but whereas in Ortiz's text the Afro-Cuban elements are recoded as evidence of *brujería,* in the novel they become images of primitivist exoticism. A different kind of evidence is uncovered by the ethnographic gaze, by means of which Afro-Cuban culture becomes a rich source for avant-garde collectors. For Ortiz, the blacks' images of African gods were crude fetishes, not Art: "two crudely made wooden dolls." But the photographs in *¡Ecué-Yamba-O!* function like those in *Documents* and *Bifur,* turning artifact into art, so that the primitive object becomes an icon of modernity.[19]

For all their ideological differences, Ortiz's positivism and Carpentier's primitivism coincide in their appropriation and display of black culture to empower their respective discourses about the Other. When Menegildo, the black protagonist of Carpentier's novel, is arrested, he is subjected to an "anthropometric exam" (examen antropométrico) during which he is photographed from various angles, he is examined, and every scar or mark is registered, cranial capacity measured, and cavities counted (145). The Other as a criminal to be fingerprinted and as an ethnographic specimen to be analyzed are two aspects of one misappropriation in *¡Ecue-Yamba-O!* as they are in *Afro-Cuban Underworld*. The Trocadéro Museum was a place that confiscated the Other's treasures, like the police, and subjected them

---

18. Ortiz, *Hampa afro-cubana,* 24, 41–42.

19. Hal Foster notes that the early moderns "reclaimed . . . artifact as art, abstracted it into form" in *Recodings: art, spectacle, cultural politics,* 193.

to an "anthropometric exam." Georges Henri Rivière describes this process in an article in *Documents*: "Each piece will be examined, identified, drawn, measured and described."[20] Ethnography, surrealism, and the law converge.

The primitive Otherness of blacks was a recurring theme in *Documents* and *Bifur*, as was the decadence and poverty of modern Western art forms in comparison with the vitality of popular, folk, and primitive arts. Parisian audiences' hunger for spectacle was fed by black performers like the jazz revue *Black Birds*, which was enthusiastically praised by both Bataille and Michel Leiris. Leiris explains the revue's fascination as an art form so spontaneous and fresh that it would be absurd to associate it with the institutional stuffiness of "Art" with a capital "A."[21]

André Schaeffner, an ethnographic musicologist who participated in the Dakar-Djibouti expedition along with Leiris, similarly opposes official Music (with a capital "M") as high Art to "primitive" music in a note on the *Black Birds*: "we should learn to understand as music so many things that the capital 'M' would deprive us of; music is richer than Music and not less capable of grandeur."[22]

The valorization of "low" art forms over official Art is also a recurring theme in Carpentier's journal articles, and in "Bajo el cetro del *blue*" (Under the scepter of the blues) he adds his voice to the chorus of admiration for "los Black Birds neoyorquinos." He praises the intuitive nature of their art, the "profound poetry of their blues" untainted by erudition and worn-out formulas.[23]

For Menegildo Cué in *¡Ecué-Yamba-O!* as well, music is an innate, instinctual predisposition rather than a learned skill: "The feeling of rhythm throbbed in his blood. When he beat on a decaying box or a termite-infested tree trunk, he reinvented the music of man" (33). For Schaeffner, instruments like those used by Menegildo are the proper objects of study for ethnography, for they "would vanish unobserved and unstudied if photography failed to capture their performance."[24]

20. Georges Henri Rivière, "Le Musée d'Ethnographie du Trocadéro," 36. On the function of anthropometry in ethnographic studies, see Frank Spencer, "Some Notes on the Attempt to Apply Photography to Anthropometry during the Second Half of the Nineteenth Century."

21. Michel Leiris, *Documents* 4 (1929): 222.

22. André Schaeffner, *Documents* 4 (1929): 223. Schaeffner's note on the *Black Birds* appears directly below a photograph of tribal Africans.

23. Carpentier, *Obras completas* 9: 156.

24. André Schaeffner, "Des Instruments de Musique dans un Musée d'Ethnographie." González Echevarría has suggested that Schaeffner may have been a model for the ethnomu-

Carpentier's portrayal of Afro-Cuban culture in *¡Ecué-Yamba-O!* is prefigured in an article he published in *Bifur* called "Lettre des Antilles." The letter from exotic places was a regular feature of *Bifur*; for example, "Lettre de Suède," "Lettre de Syrie," "Lettre d'Estonie," "Lettre d'Amérique," and even "Lettre sur Paris." In the article Carpentier, speaking as both native informant to a European audience and as detached ethnographic observer, focuses on the exotic aspects of black culture in Cuba—sorcery, rites of possession, *ñáñigo* groups. He speaks of attending magical ceremonies and of being given a prayer—magical emblem of an Other world—by a certain sorcerer. That this "Prayer to the just judge" (Prière au juste juge) that appears in the "Lettre" as well as in *¡Ecué-Yamba-O!* is also quoted word for word in Ortiz suggests that Carpentier's need to authorize his position as native informant leads him to plagiarize Ortiz.[25] Carpentier's concern for the authority of firsthand observer participation is evident as well in a letter he sent to Alejandro García Caturla in which he requests "as soon as possible" precise details concerning *ñáñigo* funeral rites that he knows Caturla to have witnessed and that he deems necessary for the writing of several chapters of *¡Ecué-Yamba-O!*[26]

The urgency of Carpentier's request for documentary evidence, like his borrowing from Ortiz, reflects his use of a rhetorical stance that James Clifford identifies as "the predominant mode of modern fieldwork authority . . . 'You are there . . . because I was there.'"[27] The use of native Afro-Cuban terms and the photographs of religious images, symbols, and practices included in the text reinforce the narrator's claim to authority. But the gaze of the spectator may disturb the pristine authenticity of primitive autonomy; while Carpentier is symbolically empowered by the sorcerer's prayer, the allegory of empowerment he recounts in the "Lettre" is undercut by one of invasion and betrayal. In "El recuerdo de Amadeo Roldán" (The memory of Amadeo Roldán) he recalls attending *ñáñigo* ceremonies together with Roldán in order to appropriate the blacks' music for use in their own compositions. Unfortunately their indiscrete writing at the scene provokes the wrath of the Other, who insists that they stop writing or leave.[28]

---

sicologist protagonist of *Los pasos perdidos* (1953) and notes that Carpentier corresponded with Schaeffner. See his *Myth and Archive*, 16 and 189*n15*.

25. Carpenter, "Lettre des Antilles," 93–94; *¡Ecué-Yamba-O!*, 26–27; *Hampa afro-cubana*, 54–56.

26. Carpentier, *Obras completas* 1: 293.

27. Clifford, *Predicament of Culture*, 22.

28. Carpentier, *Obras completas* 9: 424.

This anecdote, whose purpose is to remember and memorialize Roldán on the occasion of his death, is subliminally a story about collecting as a guilty activity. For Schaeffner, the ephemeral nature of primitive instruments meant that without the ethnographer's camera they would be consigned to oblivion. Carpentier's writing, like the ethnographer's camera, attempts to entrap the ephemeral, spontaneous performance of the primitive in a mechanically reproducible form for a European audience. Writing thus becomes a tool used by the colonizer to disinherit and corrupt the colonized.[29]

In the "Lettre," Carpentier describes at length the black *ñáñigo* groups as well as the Chinese *tongs* active in Havana. He shared with Bataille a fascination for secret societies; in the 1956 letter to Bataille, he recalls conversations they had in 1929 or 1930 about secret societies in Cuba.[30] European intellectuals were attracted to secret societies for their devotion to what modern Western civilization had lost: a sense of community, usually based on fanatic group loyalty, a secret language and arcane initiation rites, and a religious, magical connection with the world.

Another aspect of these groups that contributed to their exotic appeal was their status as beyond the law. Outlawed by the police, both the *ñáñigo* groups and the *tongs* formed part of the criminal underworld of Havana. The surrealists were attracted to those who lived on the fringes of society—the homeless ("clochards"), the criminals, the prostitutes. These marginal types constituted their own secret societies, having their own rules, their own slang, their own codes of honor and retribution. The French, notes Brassaï, "out of curiosity, a yen for low-life, were drawn to the Rue de Lappe, even the bourgeois from Passy and the aristocrats from the Faubourg Saint-Germain."[31]

Both the *ñáñigo* groups and the *tongs* are based on male bonding; the founding gesture of the *ñáñigo* subculture as recounted by Carpentier in the "Lettre" as well as in *¡Ecué-Yamba-O!* is the murder of a woman who had too much knowledge of their secrets. The primordial values of these

29. José Piedra discusses the conflicts involved in the appropriation and textualization of Afro-Cuban oral and ritual performances as they are dramatized self-consciously in Carpentier's early works. In "The Afro-Cuban Esthetics of Alejo Carpentier."

30. In the late 1930s, Bataille, along with Leiris and Roger Caillois, founded the "Collège de Sociologie," a group devoted to studying manifestations of the sacred in modern life, among which they counted secret societies. See Denis Hollier, ed., *The College of Sociology 1937–39*.

31. Brassaï, *The Secret Paris of the 30s*, n.p. Brassaï's photographic homage to the Parisian underworld, *Paris de nuit*, was published in 1933.

groups are courage, virility, and loyalty: "they will become his enemies if he betrays them, if he reveals their secrets."[32]

That revealing secrets is the lowest thing that a member of a secret society can do reveals Carpentier's rhetorical position to be fraught with contradictions. His desire to show himself an insider, which leads him to divulge the text of the "Prière au juste juge" given to him by a sorcerer (in his own account) and to transcribe a *tong* document that had been seized by the police,[33] brands him as inexorably an outsider and a traitor—a betrayer of secrets, an "enemy."

Mary Louise Pratt has noted that in eighteenth-century travel writing on the ¡Kung a portrait of the colonized Other emerges:

> they acquire the characteristics that the powerful commonly find in those they have subjugated: meekness, innocence, passivity, indolence coupled with physical strength and stamina, cheerfulness, absence of greed or indeed desires of any kind, internal egalitarianism, a penchant for living in the present, inability to take initiatives on their own behalf.[34]

Carpentier characterizes the Cuban black in the "Lettre" in a remarkably similar vein: "The black Cuban of the countryside is sweet, optimistic and lazy . . . he dances in the sun." He praises their ability to adapt, in essence their malleability: "When one speaks of blacks, one almost always fails to take into account their power to adapt to new milieus, their ability to transform themselves on the spot, to create new traditions."[35] This mutability, this chameleonlike lack of a stable cultural identity, is a projection of Western discourse about the colonized Other as "a nullity . . . [that] reflects any desire."

According to Christopher Miller, Africanist discourse, or European discourse about Africa and Africans, is constituted by the perception of an *absence* and a sense that the colonized Other will never be fully a subject for Europe, but always a "copy," a being constituted by difference in conflict with his desire to be the same: "Across the gap between Europe and the black world, the traffic is imitation, parody, and desire for sameness."[36]

32. Carpentier, "Lettre des Antilles," 100.
33. Carpentier, "Lettre des Antilles," 104.
34. Mary Louise Pratt, "Fieldwork in Common Places," 46.
35. Carpentier, "Lettre des Antilles," 92, 91.
36. Christopher Miller, *Blank Darkness: Africanist Discourse in French*, 49, 24.

In *¡Ecué-Yamba-O!* Havana is *like* Paris in its shop windows, its exotic collage culture, and the invasion of its landscape by advertising:

> Antonio led Menegildo and Longina toward the business district, where clerks were napping behind their counters, between percales and organdies. . . . Sweets were melting in their jars; shirts were fading behind glass windows.

> (Antonio condujo a Menegildo y Longina hacia la calle comercial, donde los dependientes dormitaban detrás de sus mostradores, entre percalinas y organdíes. . . . Los confites se derretían en sus pomos; las camisas se descolorían tras de las vidrieras.) (164)

Although Havana here *resembles* Paris, it becomes rather a mimetic displacement with striking incongruities: "the clerks *were napping*," "the sweets *were melting*," "the shirts *were fading*" (emphasis added). There is a kind of slippage or displacement here that underscores the distance between Paris and its colonial imitator, and the ironies that occur when the center exports its products to the periphery. Critics of *¡Ecué-Yamba-O!* have noted the contrast between Menegildo Cué's rural home—cosmic, earthbound, ritual-oriented, primitive, authentically Cuban—and the corruption of the modern city, where alienation rules.[37] But there has been no discussion of Carpentier's portrayal of the colonial city as a parodic "copy" of Europe in his first novel. Roberto González Echevarría associates parody with Carpentier's later work, as in his 1974 *El recurso del método* (*Reasons of State*) where the city becomes "a stage for comic opera" with no stable identity behind the "props" of its successive "productions": "the city is decorated with painted palm trees and other props. The view of the city is here . . . that of a stage set, one of such monumental proportions that it can only evoke the opera."[38] The illusion of order propped up by an aging dictator in *El recurso* gives way in *Concierto barroco* (1974), according to González Echevarría, to a vision of Latin America's symbiotic relation with Europe as a synchretic disorder without origins that only produces infinite mutations and distortions.

Although González Echevarría finds parody absent in *¡Ecué-Yamba-O!*, Carpentier's perception of Latin America as a distorted mirror image of Europe originates in his first novel and is related to his own anxiety about

---

37. See González Echevarría's Spenglerian interpretation in *The Pilgrim at Home*, 34–96.
38. González Echevarría, *The Pilgrim at Home*, 265.

originality vis-à-vis Europe. In an article published in *Carteles* in 1931, Carpentier expresses his concern about Latin American writers' belated and mimetic relation to European letters:

> In Latin America, enthusiasm for what is European has given rise to a certain spirit of imitation that has had the deplorable consequence of retarding by many years our own native expression . . . We've dreamed of Versailles . . . while Indians were telling their marvellous legends in our own backyard and we didn't want to see it . . . [39]

In the Havana of *¡Ecué-Yamba-O!* theatrical performers skilled in the art of imitation abound. Menegildo finds a job as protagonist of a freak show where the circus acts are performed by rather disheveled, down-and-out versions of circus performers: "In the afternoon, a parade made up of a *dirty* elephant, a camel with a *fallen hump* . . . acrobats dressed in *faded tights,* made its way through the main street" (Por la tarde, una parada, integrada por un elefante *sucio,* un camello *con la giba caída* . . . acróbatas vestidos de *mallas descoloridas,* recorrió la calle principal, 201; emphasis added). Menegildo's role allows his dramatic abilities—his capacity for imitation—to shine, as he plays the part of a beheader of saints "with an absolute conviction" that "demonstrated a talent for drama" that took Antonio by surprise (202).[40]

This same propensity for imitation can be seen as well in Crescencio, a boarder at the *Solar de La Lipidia* where Menegildo and his lover Longina make their home, together with an assortment of low-life characters pretending to be what they are not: "bricklayers without work, politickers without candidates, dance bands without a dance" ([a]lbañiles 'sin pega', politiqueros sin candidato, soneros faltos de baile, 168). Crescencio is a would-be opera singer who lives "waiting for the day he can set off for Milan to 'develop his voice' and sing *Otello* at La Scala" (en espera del día en que embarcara para Milán con el fin de 'desarrollar la vó' y cantar *Oteyo* en la Escala, 168–69). One night his boisterous pseudo-version of a Verdi aria—"lan dona emobile, cuá pluma viento"—elicits this irritated response from a fellow boarder: "he hasn't looked in the mirror, and he

---

39. Carpentier, "América ante la joven literatura europea," 55.

40. Menegildo's circus performance can be compared to the performances of natives at late-nineteenth- and early-twentieth-century European Exhibitions like those attended and described by Carpentier in his *crónicas.* On native performances at these shows, see Brian Street, "British Popular Anthropology: Exhibiting and Photographing the Other."

wants to speak Italian" (¡No se ha mirao en el ep'pejo, y quiere hablal en italiano!, 170). Crescencio's desire to be the same (as a European model) only produces difference as parody as the implied reader of Carpentier's novel recognizes the distance between Crescencio's botched version of Verdi and the original.[41]

Another character with a vocation for mimicry is an unwanted guest at Cristalina Valdés's "spiritist center" (centro espiritista): "The atmosphere would just get right to receive messages from the other side when the intruder would pretend to fall into a trance, spoiling a performance Cristalina had been working on for days" (Apenas el ambiente se hacía propicio para acoger los mensajes de la orilla obscura, la intrusa fingía caer en trance, echando a perder un trabajo preparado por Cristalina durante varios días, 200). Atilana's "pretensions to being a medium" (pretensiones a la mediumnidad), like Crescencio's operatic pretensions, are gestures that constitute the colonized Other as an imposter with mimetic desires revealed by the ironic narrator to be unrealizable.

The city evoked by Carpentier in *¡Ecué-Yamba-O!* is characterized by multiplicity, promiscuity, prostitution, and mimicry. The many businesses take their names from French cultural icons: "The Versailles Café with its coconut pyramids and its window coated with flies. The Louvre, whose entrance was reserved for shoeshiners" (El *Café de Versailles,* con sus pirámides de cocos y su vidriera llena de moscas. *El Louvre,* cuyo portal era feudo de limpiabotas, 142). They sell imported products: "sardines caught in Terranova, peaches in cans named for some romantic novel" (sardinas pescadas en Terranova, albaricoques encerrados en latas con nombre de novela romántica, 129). Even the prostitutes are readers of Pierre Loti (153).

The city is a vortex of inauthenticity that draws Menegildo with its circuslike attractions and immediate gratifications: "Here is where you have a good time!" (¡Aquí e donde se gosa!) he remarks enthusiastically to Longina. The black Menegildo is infinitely corruptible because infinitely malleable— a nullity. Cuba's "difference," like Menegildo's, is menaced by its empty disposition toward mimicry. To conserve its Otherness, Carpentier seems

41. Havana here curiously resembles Brassaï's nocturnal view of Paris, with its street fairs, circuses, and strange characters like the madam of the Suzy brothel who loved opera and the German-born Hollywood stuntman—"The Human Gorilla"—and his music-hall-dancer wife, who lived "in a hotel for acrobats not far from the Cirque Médrano. Everyone there was either a magician, a trapeze artist, or a snake charmer." *The Secret Paris of the 30s,* n.p.

to suggest, is to renounce prostituting itself to European models; the black's authenticity, and by extension that of Cuba, is contingent on remaining pure: "The bongo drum, antidote to Wall Street!" (¡El bongó, antídoto de Wall-Street!, 129). This authentic African presence is the antidote as well for the slavish imitation of European letters.

In a chapter entitled "Fiesta" a circus and a Salvation Army group become competing spectacles:

> The passersby had grouped together to watch a Jamaican woman singing hymns accompanied by two big black men sporting Salvation Army caps . . .
> . . . And the wave of spectators turned suddenly toward a nearby street where a hurdy-gurdy man was playing *Poeta y aldeano* . . .
> Come see the fire-eating Indian! The strongest woman in the world! Today is the last day!
> Given this urgency, God's train had to take off with four sweaty Jamaicans as its only passengers.
>
> (Los transeúntes se habían agrupado para ver a una jamaiquina que entonaba himnos religiosos, acompañada por dos negrazos que exhibían las gorras de la Salvation Army . . .
> . . . Y toda la oleada de espectadores rodó bruscamente hacia una calle cercana. El organillo eléctrico del *Silco* tocaba la obertura de *Poeta y aldeano* . . .
> ¡Entren a ver el indio comecandela! ¡La mujel má fuelte del mundo! ¡El hombre ejqueleto . . . ! ¡Hoy é el último día . . . !
> Ante este imperativo de fechas, el ferrocarril del Señor tuvo que partir con cuatro jamaiquinas sudorosas por todo pasaje.) (70–72)

Here the Jamaicans imitating a Salvation Army corps are implicitly compared to the sideshows in the circus. The blacks wearing Salvation Army caps are as exotic as the "fire-eating Indian" (indio comecandela) or the "skeleton man" (hombre ejqueleto). Carpentier underscores the parodic aspect of the scene:

> It was an unexpected version of the scene one can see every Sunday in the dirtiest and foggiest streets of Saxon cities. The sister was inviting the crowd to enter the temple with enticing gestures that made one think of those offered at the entrance to brothels . . .
>
> (Era una inesperada versión de la escena a que se asiste, cada domingo, en las calles más sucias y neblinosas de las ciudades sajonas. La *hermana* invitaba a los presentes a penetrar en el templo, con esos

ademanes prometedoras que hacen pensar en los gestos prodigados
a la entrada de los burdeles . . . ) (71)

That the Jamaican woman intoning religious hymns resembles a prostitute is a function of the narrator's ironic imagination that presents the
scene as an other-voiced replica of an original text set in "the foggy streets
of Saxon cities." By extension, Cuba *prostitutes itself* when it becomes a
circuslike "version" of a European norm. The setting of these scenes of
parodic mimicry in the city, in Havana, determines the manner in which
they may be read. In *¡Ecué-Yamba-O!* there are two Cubas: an exotic, rural
one where blacks and *guajiros* (country people) conserve their originality
in the synchretic creation of Afro-Cuban culture in spite of their colonial
condition; and Havana, which pretends to be a copy of a European city in
vain. The urban *flâneur's* attraction to the dynamic heterogeneity of the
city, its spectacles, and its budding commercialism has its counterpoint,
then, in the novelist's nostalgia for a specifically *criollo* rural reality that
the rise of the city will undermine and refashion.[42]

Carpentier's ironic imagination does not coincide with current poststructuralist views of mimicry as a subtle way of usurping colonial power,
unsettling authority by showing it a parodic mirror image of itself.[43] While
poststructuralists have focused on the disturbing ironies of colonial representations of hegemonic forms, Carpentier's perception of the same
ironic situation led him to posit an alternative form of representation that
would celebrate the hybrid condition as authentic, rather than as alienated
from some essence emanating from Europe—and that alternative form was
inspired by the decentering hybridity of collage.

If parody is produced by the infinitely deferred desire to be the same as
Europe, for Carpentier Latin America is constituted by the consciousness
of its difference, of its necessarily synchretic, hybrid nature, "the consciousness that an American develops, whether the son of a white man
from Europe, the son of a black African, or the son of an Indian born in

42. Carpentier's nostalgia for "la tierra" as the basis for establishing a specifically national
character was typical of his time. On the urban *crónica* that develops during the end of the
nineteenth century and is still going strong well into the twentieth, see Julio Ramos, "Decorar
la ciudad: *crónica* y experiencia urbana," in *Desencuentros de la modernidad en América
Latina: Literatura y política en el siglo XIX,* 112–42.

43. For an introduction to Homi Bhabha's writings on colonialism and mimicry in the
context of poststructuralism, see Robert Young, *White Mythologies: Writing History and the
West,* 141–56.

America . . . of being something other, something new, a symbiosis."[44] In the "Lettre" Carpentier praises the talent of the Cuban black for refashioning himself, remaking himself in the New World. He celebrates the hybridity of synchretic Afro-Cuban culture and rejects mimicry and imitation as a perversion that later produces that monstrous paradigmatic "mimic man" Henri Christophe in his 1949 novel *El reino de este mundo* (*The Kingdom of This World*).

As Christopher Miller suggests, the black is for the West a malleable figure that "reflects any desire." He is at once "sweet, optimistic and lazy"—a naive innocent—and at the same time a violent, tragic figure of the underworld. He is the passive object of ethnographic scrutiny, and a powerful sorcerer. As a figure of Carpentier's desire to be original and not a copy of Europe, the black fashions Afro-Cuban culture out of the heterogeneous elements that come to hand, like a *bricoleur,* as an autochthonous version of surrealist collage.

In *¡Ecué-Yamba-O!* meanwhile, Carpentier begins to see and suggest what he apparently cannot see or say about the Colonial Exposition: that viewing cultural pastiche as aesthetic spectacle conceals colonial relations of power and subjugation. There is no trace of judgment in Carpentier's celebratory articles on the Exposition, despite the fact that mainstream surrealists boycotted it and expressed their anticolonialist views in "Ne visitez pas l'Exposition Coloniale" (Don't visit the Colonial Exposition).[45] In an article published in *Bifur,* Félicien Challaye denounced the Exposition's premises, noting that France portrayed its mission as marked by the generosity of spirit with which it was bringing its superior forms of civilization to the colonies, which presumably benefited in all ways from such contact with French culture. Challaye points out that this official version served to mask the exploitation that characterized the colonial situation.[46]

It seems unlikely that Carpentier was unaware of such widespread anti-Exposition sentiments. Perhaps while the persona he adopted in the *Carteles* and *Social* articles precluded all but aesthetic commentary, in the novel the contradictions and ironies of his position became harder to manage as a narrative involving colonial lives and histories displaced the disengaged surrealist aesthetics of the *flâneur.* In any case, Carpentier's subsequent need to disavow his only "ethnographic-surrealist" novel

44. Carpentier, *La novela latinoamericana,* 126.
45. In Eric Losfield, ed., *Tracts surréalistes et déclarations collectives,* 194–95.
46. Félicien Challaye, "Souvenirs sur la colonisation," 43.

cannot be completely divorced from feelings of guilt and treachery.[47] A suggestion that this is so can be found in *Los pasos perdidos* (1953), which chronicles the unmasking of a former ethnographic-surrealist as a *poseur,* and in *El acoso* (1958), an obsessive and tragic account of betrayal and retribution.

Although Carpentier repudiated surrealism in constituting "the marvelous real," the surrealist-ethnographic connection that he established during his years in Paris proved a fertile ground for his imagination, and collage becomes a model for the lush intricacies that characterize his later baroque style. What sets Carpentier's vision of collage and the baroque apart from its surrealist origins (as the marvelous real from the *merveilleux*) is his feeling that the juxtaposition of the incongruous is already inscribed in the landscape and the social relations of Latin America, whereas surrealists sought to create these effects in order to disrupt the West's perception of itself as a seamless whole. Carpentier reinvents the Frazerian comparativism he inherits from Ortiz, replotting its evolutionary schema as one of simultaneity; that is, rather than view *ñáñigo* ceremonies as the endpoint of a tradition derived from Greek tragedy, as did Ortiz, he views the two rituals as existing together, melded in the same ritual act as symbiotic creations: as collage.

47. Carpentier's repudiation of *¡Ecué-Yamba-O!* has been widely quoted. See for example González Echevarría, *The Pilgrim at Home,* 63.

# 3

## THE EYE OF THE ANTHROPOLOGIST
### Vision and Mastery in José María Arguedas

The science of anthropology has traditionally involved closely observing other cultures in order to accumulate data and develop knowledge about them.[1] The anthropologist, an outsider viewing the native dispassionately from a certain distance, positions himself in the field to collect information based on firsthand observation that supposedly guarantees scientific objectivity, while precluding more intimate, subjective involvement. As an ethnographer, the Peruvian writer José María Arguedas had to conform to some extent to this paradigm for producing knowledge, which he nevertheless found inadequate to translate his personal experience of Andean reality.[2] The lyrical tone of Arguedas's ethnographic writings attests to, in William Rowe's words, "a passionate approach to the object of study" in sharp contrast to the science of ethnography's traditional methods for producing and reporting knowledge.[3]

Arguedas's attraction to alternative ways of knowing derived from an Andean worldview leads him to celebrate music in his writing as the vehicle for a transcendent mode of knowledge. But while critics have

1. According to James Clifford, "The predominant metaphors in anthropological research have been participant-observation, data collection, and cultural description, all of which presuppose a standpoint outside—looking at, objectifying, or, somewhat closer, 'reading,' a given reality," Clifford and Marcus, eds., *Writing Culture*, 11.

2. On the difficulties of translating one cultural code into another in the Andean context, see Regina Harrison's *Signs, Songs, and Memory in the Andes*.

3. William Rowe, "Arguedas: música, conocimiento y transformación social," 98.

written extensively on music as a utopian element in Arguedas's work, the question of the visual and the problem of viewing the Other, which the writer returns to consistently in his fiction and in his anthropological essays, has been largely ignored. The visual as the primary mode of perception in scientific observation places the observer in a hierarchical position of dominance over the observed. Although he would reject the mastery that this implies, I will argue that in Arguedas's work there is a subliminal, repressed attraction to the power of the gaze to capture and dominate the elusive Other.

Angel Rama has suggested that music functions as a transculturizing element in *Los ríos profundos* (*Deep Rivers*), undermining and at the same time enriching the novel as a form. Arguedas uses music both on the level of structure (using repetition and analogy in place of the logical progression of a realist plot, inserting Indian songs that form a counterpoint to the text's more traditional narrative elements) and in a generally lyrical approach to words that, according to Rama, "are spoken, intoned, perceived as sounds and rarely seen as written."[4] The novel, he claims, actually "sings" for the reader, is orchestrated rather than written in the traditional sense. Through music, Arguedas evokes and celebrates a logic derived from Indian modes of thought that is antithetical to the rational strictures of a Western worldview that underlie the realist novel. As an expression of the popular classes, music generates collective experiences that transcend the isolation of the individual, and thus directly responds to the forces of modernization and the alienation of the individual that result from the breakdown of traditional societies. In Rama's view, music expresses the inner (transculturizing) logic of the novel itself, as in song the traditional (Indian music) and emerging (*mestizo* lyrics) elements of Peruvian culture come together in a creative fusion.

For William Rowe, as for Rama, music in Arguedas becomes a way of knowing that opposes itself to Western rationalism. He contrasts visual and aural modes of perception, categorizing the visual as the privileged mode of Western rationalism and science: "sight dissects reality, a propensity that is given a positive valuation in the rationalist philosophy of Descartes." If Western knowledge is founded on the distance or separation between knower and known, music is for Rowe a utopian force that transcends individual isolation and separation through collective moments

4. Angel Rama, *Transculturación narrativa*, 253. *Los ríos profundos* was originally published in 1958 and was translated as *Deep Rivers* in 1978.

of intensity in ritual dance and song: "Arguedas's music transcends that division, dismantling the repressive codification of existence . . . Against capitalist alienation and reification, self and world are united."[5]

In Arguedas, music often creates a kind of incandescence, a flash of illumination during which the diverse elements of the universe speak through the music, are distilled and integrated in an epiphanic return to wholeness against the forces of fragmentation:

> The smoke from the factories, the shouting of the fruitsellers . . . the flow of passing buses and tricycles . . . the parade of fishermen coming from the docks . . . the barking of dogs . . . all this was blended and set glowing when Crispín Antolín played his guitar . . .
>
> (El humo de las fábricas, el griterío de los vendedores de fruta . . . el flujo de los colectivos y triciclos . . . el desfile . . . de los pescadores que se iban del muelle . . . el ladrido de los perros . . . todo eso se constreñía, también como relampagueando, en la guitarra de Crispín Antolín . . . )[6]

Rowe asserts that in Arguedas's writing, the sense of sight becomes subordinate to sound and partakes of its transforming, liberating powers. He cites a passage from *El zorro de arriba y el zorro de abajo* (Fox from above and fox from below, 1971) in which a moment of visual intensity functions in the same way in which such musical moments do: "those lice became illuminated, became transparent, showing their guts by the light of the *pariwana*'s wings, more intimate and far off than that of the sun . . . that image transformed our life into music" (esos piojos se iluminaban, se hacían transparentes, mostraban sus tripitas con la luz de las alas de la *pariwana,* más íntima y lejana que la del sol . . . esa imagen convertía en música toda nuestra vida).[7] Just as the essence of the world can be distilled and heard in intense, epiphanic musical moments, it can be seen, made transparent in a flash of revelation, as in this euphoric description of a tree in *Fox from Above and Fox from Below*:

> A tree like these . . . knows of all there is under the ground and in the skies. It knows what stars are made of and what all the different types of roots, waters, insects, birds and worms are made of; and

5. Rowe, "Arguedas," 105, 107.
6. José María Arguedas, *El zorro de arriba y el zorro de abajo*, 87.
7. Rowe, "Arguedas," 106.

that knowledge is transmitted directly by the sound its trunk emits . . . as music, wisdom, solace, immortality. If you stand away from these immense solitary trees their image retains all those truths . . .

(Un árbol de éstos . . . sabe de cuanto hay debajo de la tierra y en los cielos. Conoce la materia de los astros, de todos los tipos de raíces y aguas, insectos, aves y gusanos; y ese conocimiento se transmite directamente en el sonido que emite su tronco . . . a manera de música, de sabiduría, de consuelo, de inmortalidad. Si te alejas un poco de estos inmensos solitarios ya es su imagen la que contiene todas esas verdades . . . )[8]

But although clearly there are these epiphanic, utopistic moments of illumination in Arguedas's novels, it is wrong to extrapolate a poetics based on these scenes alone. For the novels are full of dark, as well as uplifting, epiphanies. I will argue that unlike music, which as these and other critics suggest was certainly articulated in utopian terms by Arguedas, the visual was a rather more conflicted mode of perception for the writer. He perceived the act of looking in fact not as an innocent, and not as a consistently uplifting, activity, but rather as one fraught with issues of control, mastery, pleasure, pain, and guilt. In this chapter I discuss the ways in which Arguedas problematizes the visual in his work; first, in a persistent focus on the act of viewing others; and second, by repeatedly foregrounding certain associations: that of viewing from above with power and mastery, and that of viewing from a distance with alienation, or with voyeurism and sadism. I will argue that Arguedas's ethnographic focus on the Other became a way for him to purge the negative, potentially alienating effects of the erotics of viewing that create disorder in his texts, and to transcend the traumatic isolation of the individual gaze.

In Arguedas's fictional world, relations of power and status are revealed by the way in which one character looks at another. The aggressive stare of the landowner Don Ciprián in "Los escoleros" (The schoolboys), for example, reflects his position of dominance: "Don Ciprián is like Satan! . . . His gaze alone makes chickens of the *comuneros*!" (¡Don Ciprián es como satanás! . . . ¡Su mirar nomás engallina a los comuneros!).[9] In *Deep Rivers* the narrator Ernesto relates how the old man who humiliates his father in Cuzco looks at him "as if he were trying to make me sink into the rug"

8. Arguedas, *El zorro*, 194.
9. José María Arguedas, *Relatos completos,* 106.

(como intentando hundirme en la alfombra).[10] The old man's servant, on the other hand, is so humble and self-effacing that he refuses to meet Ernesto's eyes (5; 9). In contrast to the abject humility of the servant or *pongo,* the *mestizo*'s expression "was . . . almost insolent" (era . . . casi insolente, 5; 9). The officers who arrive in Abancay in the wake of social unrest "looked at other people . . . with a kind of lewdness, peculiar to them alone" (miraban con una expresión de lujuria acaso exclusivo de ellos, 192–93; 211). Soldiers adopt a condescending air "as if they might be looking down on people from another planet" (contemplando a los demás desde otro mundo, 192; 210). Ernesto is scandalized by the presence in Abancay of young men who leer disrespectfully at young girls: "I was shocked by . . . the insolent glances the boys gave them" (Me chocaba[n] . . . las miradas que les dirigían, insolentes, 184; 202).

Ernesto is frightened by what he sees in Father Linares's eyes when the priest accuses him of sleeping with la Opa (210; 230). In contrast, he imagines the black Brother Miguel "would have gazed at me with his eyes that were white and mild, like those of all beings who truly love the world" (me habría mirado con sus ojos blancos y humildes, como los de todo ser que ama verdaderamente al mundo, 211; 231). In a moment of anguish, the narrator yearns for the purifying solace of his father's gaze: "[o]nly my father's blue eyes could have soothed me that night and freed me from all the evil I had seen during the day" (Sólo los ojos azules de mi padre me habrían calmado, me habrían liberado aquella noche de tanta maldad que vi durante el día, 189; 207). Instead, he is forced to endure the hostile gaze of strangers: "Many people cast inquiring glances at me" (Me miraban con extrañeza, muchos, 168; 185); "some . . . were watching me with great curiosity" (algunos me miraban con curiosidad excesiva, 183; 200).

It seems clear that for Arguedas, looking has intentionality—can be aggressive, alienating, purifying—and is implicated in social relations of power. In his writing, viewing from above comes to represent control over others. Don Fermín Aragón de Peralta in *Todas las sangres* (All the bloods, 1964) is literally lord of all he surveys in his house in the cleft of a mountainside, where "as from a condors' nest" (como desde un nido de cóndores) he could keep his eyes on the surrounding area.[11]

---

10. José María Arguedas, *Los ríos profundos,* 21; *Deep Rivers,* 17. Subsequent page references will be made parenthetically in the text, first to the version in English, then to the original.

11. José María Arguedas, *Todas las sangres,* 101.

Don Fermín's panoramic or panoptic gaze ensures his control over his mining operations. The reference to condors is not casual, as it alludes to a similar association of gazing from on high with mastery in the Andean tradition. According to Jean R. Barstow, "*Mallku,* the Aymara word for condor, is also the traditional term for male political authority." She notes that the condor's aggressive role as abductor and fighter in folklore reflects an Andean reality—that those living in the highlands have historically dominated those living at lower levels—and goes on to say that the opposition high (dominance) / low (submission) also has implications for gender roles: "The condor and the heights of the *puna* suggest maleness in Aymara thought when juxtaposed with lower elevations, which in comparison appear female."[12] While don Fermín keeps vigil from his "condor's nest," down below the crippled servant and rape victim Gertrudis "looked like an ant, she couldn't lower herself any more, reduce herself to the level of the ground" (parecía una hormiga, no podía ya agacharse más, reducirse a ras de la tierra).[13]

The Andean association of authority with vigilance from above is also related to the traditional worship of mountain gods who watch over their Indian followers, exacting tribute, punishing negligence, and rewarding service. The gaze of the mountain god Chawala in Arguedas's short story "Warma Kuyay" is so powerful that the Indians avert their eyes rather than look at him directly.[14] The penetrating male gaze of Chawala feminizes the Indians in a sense, like that of don Ciprián "makes chickens of the Indians."[15]

The imposition of the male subject's gaze onto the female object has erotic connotations, and Arguedas's position as an outsider living in close proximity to Indian culture facilitated his perception of his role as a kind of eavesdropper or voyeur.[16] The writer's obsession with the act of seeing as transgression or violation can be traced directly to a traumatic childhood experience, which he attempted to exorcise in some way in nearly

---

12. Jean R. Barstow, "Marriage between Human Beings and Animals: A Structuralist Discussion of Two Aymara Myths," 76–77.

13. Arguedas, *Todas las sangres,* 32.

14. Arguedas, *Relatos completos,* 122. For the role of mountain gods in Andean belief, see Sabine MacCormack, *Religion in the Andes: Vision and Imagination in Early Colonial Peru.*

15. The association of viewing from a distance with power and domination is thus not strictly a function of Western rationalism's separation of subject and object, as Rowe asserts.

16. The relevant facts of Arguedas's life are well known; see his comments in *Primer encuentro de narradores peruanos.*

everything he wrote. In an interview with Sara Castro Klarén, Arguedas relates how a cruel and exhibitionistic stepbrother forced him at the age of nine to be present at his sexual performances.[17] What becomes a torment for Arguedas is the desire to see, an erotic involvement with the act of seeing, that conflicts with an equally strongly felt repulsion for the same scene.[18]

The closest Arguedas comes to recreating his trauma in fiction is in the first story of *Amor mundo,* "El horno viejo" (The old furnace room). In it the innocent young boy Santiago is dragged out of bed by an older boy in order to watch him have sex with his aunt Gabriela against her will. The story narrates Santiago's introduction to sex as something degrading and bestial, but ultimately seductive in its horrific fascination. Seeing becomes for the boy a guilty, illicit but compelling act, and at the end when he is forced to leave the scene of an orgy because of the women's protests, he cannot tear himself away:

> He stayed outside . . . Sitting by the door, Santiago was looking at the light . . . what wasn't peaceful with that full moon shining from the center of the sky? Except for himself, that is. "That one is a nobody," the *señor* would say. They made him fall down when they opened the furnace room door.
>
> (Se quedó afuera . . . Sentado en la puerta, Santiago estuvo mirando la luz . . . ¿qué no estaba tranquilo con esa luna llena viniendo del centro del cielo? Menos él, el chico, pues. "No es nadie ése," decía el señor. Lo hicieron caer al abrir la puerta del horno viejo.)[19]

The initiation of the boy Santiago into the conflictive pleasures of the erotics of viewing leads him to see the Indian ritual *ayla* in remarkably similar terms. The story "El ayla" dramatizes Santiago's attempt as an outsider to view the ritual from a perspective that would not be alienating. Significantly, the ritual involves sex between unmarried young men and women who perform a fertility dance that ends with them pairing off up

17. "José María Arguedas, Testimonio sobre preguntas de Sara Castro Klarén." For an excellent essay on the impact of this early trauma in Arguedas's writing, see Mario Vargas Llosa, *José María Arguedas: entre sapos y halcones.*

18. According to Susan Sontag, these poles of fascination and repulsion are at the heart of anthropology: "always anthropology has struggled with an intense, fascinated *repulsion* toward its subject. The horror of the primitive . . . is never far from the anthropologist's consciousness." In "The Anthropologist as Hero," 190.

19. José María Arguedas, *Relatos completos,* 191.

in the mountains in an idyllic communion with nature. While in "El horno viejo" Santiago sees sex as a horrific, demonic nightmare, the same activity in "El ayla" becomes a paean to nature, transformed by the redemptive power of ritual.[20]

In the story the *Auki* or priest, who in his ceremonial role stands in for the mountain god, is empowered with a panoramic vision of the community as he witnesses the celebratory *ayla*, "reaching with his heavy eyes where the light was concentrated, the limits of all that was part of the community: mountains, valleys, abysses, summits, hawthorn forests, fields of straw, colored earth" (alcanzando con sus ojos pesados en que la luz se concentraba, todos los confines de las pertinencias de la comunidad: montes, quebradas, abismos, cumbres, bosques de espino, campos de paja, tierras de colores).[21]

Unlike the *Auki*'s, Santiago's is an erratic, fragmented perspective based on an outsider's incomplete perception of any ritual from which he is excluded. At first he follows behind the chain of dancers. When the chain breaks up, Santiago changes strategies, going ahead and reaching the plaza before the dancers. Once in the plaza, the boy climbs a tower to gaze down upon them. When the dancers leave the plaza headed for the mountain, Santiago once more follows along.[22] Although a young participant waiting for his lover tells Santiago that like all non-Indians he can't witness the *ayla*, the boy is determined to see what he can, which he does by hiding himself in the bushes and quietly taking in one young couple's performance of the ritual *ayla*'s culminating sexual act.[23]

As in "El horno viejo," Santiago insists on staying at the scene clandestinely as a voyeur, but unlike the tormented pleasure of the scurrilous orgies organized by his tormentor in the previous story, watching the *ayla* fills the boy with exaltation, elation, a feeling so euphoric that he emerges

20. The contrast between sex among whites and *mestizos* as degrading and that of the Indian ritual as purifying and life-affirming has been noted by several critics. See Vargas Llosa, *Arguedas*; Sara Castro Klarén, "Crimen y castigo: Sexualidad en José María Arguedas"; Antonio Cornejo Polar, *Los universos narrativos de José María Arguedas,* 55; Roland Forgues, *Del pensamiento dialéctico al pensamiento trágico,* 250.

21. Arguedas, *Relatos completos,* 201.

22. Angel Rama notes that the protagonist of *Los ríos profundos,* Ernesto, is propelled by the same kind of frenetic impulses. He suggests that Ernesto's frantic need to be in the fray is related to his "testimonial function" as reporter and witness. In *Transculturación narrativa,* 288.

23. Arguedas, *Relatos completos,* 204–5.

from his hiding place after the ritual has ended shouting "I am Santiago, Santiaguito!" His involvement, however peripheral, gives him an identity that counteracts the *señor*'s onerous "that one is a nobody." The ethnographic perspective purifies in a sense the boy's voyeurism, transforms it into a quasi-religious act. His elation is short-lived, however, and he soon experiences the deflation of knowing himself to be permanently and inexorably on the outside: "They left the boy alone, like a rock fallen from the sky" (Dejaron solo al muchacho, como una piedra caída del cielo).[24]

Santiago's experience of the *ayla* is a kind of portrait of the anthropologist as a young boy whose attempt to see all from every possible angle, to transcend the marginalized perspective of the individual, will resolve itself in the panoramic perspective of the story itself as figured in the *Auki*'s penetrating gaze. The narrator describes the Indian ceremony from a perspective that includes and thus transcends all marginal perspectives: that of the participants, of the "mestizos y señores," Santiago's, even the *Auki*'s. The panoramic perspective is a compensatory strategy that empowers the narrator, that allows him to overcome his alienated experience as an outsider by giving it a structure he commands, like the *Auki*, from a controlling distance.

Vincent Crapanzano has described this strategy, noting that the ethnographer has "a roving perspective, necessitated by his totalistic presentation of the events he is describing." This stance, according to Crapanzano, "assumes an invisibility that . . . [the ethnographer] cannot, of course, have."[25] Arguedas employs the "roving" or panoramic perspective in his essays on Indian rituals and ceremonies, where the eye sees all, is everywhere at once, but occludes its own presence. The anthropologist achieves with such a perspective a state of detachment, a vision of culture as order that transcends Santiago's frantic desires and torments, his voyeuristic compulsion, as he attempts to find a place for himself from which to look.

Arguedas tells another veiled portrait of the anthropologist as a young boy in "Canciones quechuas" (Quechua songs), an essay that, like many he wrote, straddles the line between autobiography and anthropology. In it, the anthropologist recounts his first and only experience as a five-year-old child of the Indian *turu pukllay,* the bullfight that is the central focus of *Yawar Fiesta* (Blood festival, 1941) and that, along with the *ayla,* was

24. Arguedas, *Relatos completos,* 205.
25. Vincent Crapanzano, "Hermes' Dilemma: The Masking of Subversion in Ethnographic Description," 53.

a ritual that haunted his imagination all his life and that he wrote about extensively in essays and in fiction.

The essay tells the curious story of a *misti* (non-Indian) child who becomes initiated into the conflictive pleasures of looking at Indian culture. The boy begins watching the bullfight from the elite vantage point he and his father the judge are accorded because of their status, a special box raised up on barriers improvised with trunks of eucalyptus trees.[26] Once again, viewing from above indicates control or power over the object of one's gaze.[27] But the child is so shaken by the dramatic spectacle that he sees, that he loses control and suffers a kind of crisis:

> I had the impression that the whole world, the mountains and the skies, the earth, were moaning, ablaze. I couldn't keep back the tears. And they took me far away from the barrier. But I went back and peered at the ceremony from behind the barriers, flanked by a crowd of Indians, who protected and consoled or encouraged me.
>
> (Yo tuve la impresión de que el mundo todo, las montañas y los cielos, la tierra, gemía, llameando. No pude contener las lágrimas. Y me sacaron de la barrera. Me llevaron lejos. Pero volví y miré a instantes la fiesta, detrás de las barreras, entre una multitud de indios que me protegían y consolaban o alentaban.)[28]

Driven from the scene by a feeling of horror, the boy is drawn back by his fascination, renouncing his privileged position from above and indulging in a kind of furtive looking. The Indians comfort him as adults comfort a child who has lived through a grueling rite of passage. But the child's crisis, loss of control, and renunciation of the superior position granted him by his social status is only half the story. For the adult Arguedas will regain mastery and authority, will counteract the childhood experience of loss of control, by mastering the authoritative discourse of anthropology:

> Later on when I took up the study of folklore at the University, although I never again had the opportunity to observe this same

26. Arguedas, *Señores e indios,* 176.

27. Mary Louise Pratt suggests that what she calls "the monarch-of-all-I-survey convention" in travel literature is a later version of the discourse of conquest that reaffirms "the relation of dominance" of he who sees over he who is seen. In "Conventions of Representation," 150. Significantly, Arguedas conjures an image of himself and his father in the role of conquistadors in "Canciones quechuas": "like the Spanish conquistadors we crossed the Andean mountains some twenty times" (Como los españoles de la conquista, atravesamos unas veinte veces las cordilleras de los Andes, 175).

28. Arguedas, *Señores e indios,* 176.

ceremony, I confirmed with my memories clarified and enlightened with subsequent information, that the *turu pukllay,* like many other ceremonies, constitutes a very eloquent demonstration of how Spanish customs were reworked by the native Quechua people, how they were transformed in the course of this reworking and became indigenous customs.

(Tiempo después, en la Universidad y, más tarde, cuando me dediqué a estudiar folklore, aunque no volví a tener oportunidad de observar esta misma fiesta, comprobé por mis recuerdos mejor esclarecidos e ilustrados con informaciones posteriores, que el *turu pukllay* (corrida de toros) aquél, como muchas otras fiestas, constituye una muestra muy elocuente acerca de cómo las costumbres españolas fueron reelaboradas por el pueblo autóctono quechua, cómo fueron transformadas en el curso de esta reelaboración y se convirtieron en indígenas.)[29]

The anthropologist of "Canciones quechuas" revisits the site of his childhood crisis and overcomes it by studying it, applying "subsequent information," retaking in a sense the position of control he had renounced.[30] Thus the same ritual that empowers the Indians to challenge their oppressors, empowers the anthropologist with the discursive mastery necessary to analyze it.

By imposing the transcendent discourse of anthropology, Arguedas presents a "controlled" version of voyeuristic viewing that when out of control becomes a pathological desire to subjugate the Other, a looking that enjoys mastery over its otherwise inaccessible object in a sadistic way.[31] The clearest example of this pathology can be seen in one of the writer's earliest short stories, "Warma Kuyay" (A child's love, 1935). The narrator of the story is a young boy, Ernesto, who develops an impossible love for the Indian woman Justina, several years his senior and in love with Kutu. The story becomes a tragedy for the young lovers when Kutu learns that don Froilán has raped Justina. Critics have found in this story a tender tragedy

29. Arguedas, *Señores e indios,* 177.

30. James Clifford identifies this rhetorical strategy with what he calls the "fables of rapport" of classic ethnographies that "normally portray the ethnographer's early ignorance, misunderstanding, lack of contact—frequently a sort of childlike status within the culture. In the *Bildunggeschichte* of the ethnography these states of innocence or confusion are replaced by adult, confident, disabused knowledge." In *Predicament of Culture,* 40.

31. According to Sander Gilman, a text "is an attempt to provide an image of control." He adds: "The fictional world as structured by the author is the world under control, in which even the loss of control is reduced to the level of a fiction directed and formed by the author." In *Difference and Pathology: Stereotypes of Sexuality, Race, and Madness,* 27.

of an innocent boy's love—a "warma kuyay"—for an Indian woman and his initiation into a world of violence and discrimination. Antonio Cornejo Polar discusses Ernesto's "double marginality": rejected by the Indian world he feels drawn to, he is nevertheless unwilling to embrace the white world into which he was born, yet he is unable to escape its hold over his psyche.[32] There is, however, a much more sinister level to "Warma Kuyay." What happens is that the narrator is spurned by Justina: "Leave me be, boy, go to your *señoritas!*" (¡Déjame, niño, anda donde tus señoritas!). He is rejected by her friends, who make fun of the boy: "they held hands and began to dance in a circle, to the music of Julio the guitarist. They turned around sometimes to look at each other, and laughed. I stayed outside the circle, ashamed, forever defeated" (Se agarraron de las manos y empezaron a bailar en ronda, con la musiquita de Julio el charanguero. Se volteaban a ratos, para mirarse, y reían. Yo me quedé fuera del círculo, avergonzado, vencido para siempre).[33]

The narrator's reaction to this humiliation is to gain control, which he does by climbing an old windmill and from his position on high looking down on his tormentors. The narrator turns his defeat into victory once he is able to see Justina as a "little black spot" (puntito negro, 89) from his vantage point, for immediately after this scene of empowerment, we learn that Justina has been raped by don Froilán.[34] By having Justina raped, the narrator in effect manages her inaccessibility, punishes her for it. The narrator then invites Kutu to join him in punishing the deviant woman: "Kutu! Better if we kill her off, shall we?" (¡Kutu! Mejor la mataremos los dos a ella ¿quieres?, 92).

Ernesto is scandalized that Kutu does not kill his sweetheart or avenge her by killing don Froilán. Instead, the Indian relieves his anger vicariously by lashing out pitilessly at don Froilán's animals, a scene that Ernesto is drawn to with erotic fascination:

32. Antonio Cornejo Polar, "El sentido de la narrativa de Arguedas," 50–53.

33. Arguedas, *Relatos completos,* 121. Subsequent references to this story will be made within the text.

34. The significance of this chidren's game and the narrator's positioning of himself above the players is underscored in Emilia Romero de Valle's discussion of "las rondas" in "Juegos infantiles tradicionales en el Perú," 329. She notes that the game originally had a symbolic significance: the players represented the sun, moon, and stars, and they sang and danced to praise God. The narrator symbolically takes for himself the position of the God being worshipped, counteracting on an imaginary level his felt impotence in the schema of everyday life.

At night we went into the animal pen; we picked the most delicate calves; Kutu spit on his hands, grasped the whip and lacerated the backs of the animals. And I? I sat in a corner and enjoyed it. I enjoyed it.

(En las noches entrábamos, ocultándonos, al corral; escogíamos los becerros más finos, los más delicados; Kutu se escupía en las manos, empuñaba duro el zurriago, y les rajaba el lomo a los torillitos . . . ¿Y yo? Me sentaba en un rincón y gozaba. Yo gozaba.) (92)

The sadistic pleasure Ernesto derives from watching Kutu lacerate the animals is like the pleasure of punishing Justina by having her raped (both the animal victim Zarinacha and Justina have black eyes). In a way, the narrator enjoys Justina's rape vicariously through watching Zarinacha's torment. Finally, Ernesto takes pity on the animals and drives Kutu away. Thus he has Justina raped (through don Froilán) while his rival is feminized, dispossessed, and cast off. The narrator in fact seems to despise Kutu more than he does the rapist, don Froilán. For on Kutu he projects his rage at his own impotence: "I despised Kutu; his tiny yellow coward's eyes made me tremble with rage" (Despreciaba al Kutu; sus ojos amarillos, chiquitos, cobardes, me hacían temblar de rabia, 92).

In Justina and Kutu, Arguedas projects his conflictive feelings about the Indian. Justina is idealized, and the world she represents is what the narrator loves—"the Indian ceremonies, the harvests, the planting to music and *jarawi* . . . that green valley full of the loving heat of the sun" (las fiestas indias, las cosechas, las siembras con música y *jarawi* . . . esa quebrada verde y llena del calor amoroso del sol, 94). Kutu, on the other hand, represents what repulsed Arguedas about the Indian, his abject, humble behavior, his inevitable corruption by the white world, even his appearance: "I looked at him up close; his flattened nose, his nearly oblique eyes, his thin lips blackened by coca" (le miré de cerca; su nariz aplastada, sus ojos casi oblicuos, sus labios delgados, ennegrecidos por la coca, 91). Nevertheless, the impotent Kutu who takes his rage out vicariously, sadistically, is the narrator's double; for the story is a compensatory strategy by which Arguedas, through the narrator, gains for himself the satisfaction denied him by "Justina" in the world outside his text.

In the end the narrator, having banished his rival, achieves his desire for control:

I alone stayed at don Froilán's side, but near Justina, my ungrateful little Justina. I wasn't unhappy. By the edge of that frothy river hearing the song of the ringdoves and the *tuyas,* I lived without hope; but she was under the same sky I was in that same valley that I grew up in. Watching her black eyes, hearing her laugh, gazing at her from afar, I was almost happy . . . I knew that she would belong to another, a grown man who could use a whip, who swore and fought with whiplashes at carnivals.

(Yo, solo, me quedé junto a don Froilán, pero cerca de Justina, de mi Justinacha ingrata. Yo no fui desgraciado. A la orilla de ese río espumoso, oyendo el canto de las torcazas y de las *tuyas,* yo vivía sin esperanzas; pero ella estaba bajo el mismo cielo que yo, en esa misma quebrada que fue mi nido. Contemplando sus ojos negros, oyendo su risa, mirándola desde lejitos, era casi feliz . . . sabía que tendría que ser de otro, de un hombre grande, que manejara ya zurriago, que echara ajos roncos y peleara a látigos en los carnavales.) (94)

Here the narrator, despite what he says, has established control over his victim: "gazing at her from afar," "she was under the same sky I was." The rape seems forgotten as if it had never happened, and the boy has reinvented the relation between himself, Justina, and don Froilán as a kind of pristine utopia in which she is, against all evidence, free to love another.

If the desire to punish women for their inaccessibility were unique to this story, then it might be unfair to see in the narrative a strategy by which the narrator manages textually the Other who cannot be managed outside the text. This is not the case, however. In "El vengativo" (The vengeful one), don Silvestre kills a woman in his rage at finding out that she had seduced his Indian servant Tomascha. Don Silvestre claims to exert complete control over the Indians: "The Indians always obey me like slaves" (Los indios siempre me obedecen como esclavos).[35] The woman, on the other hand, escapes his control; her sexuality is not a domain he fully commands except by force.

The *señor* reclaims power over the deviant female, once again, by making her his victim. And once again his dominance is signaled by his view of her from above, in this case from up above the *molle* trees (36). The *señor*'s desire to kill the woman is explicitly related to his desire to possess her sexually, and her murder closely resembles a rape:

I yanked the knife from my belt and went toward her with slow firm steps. She dragged herself on her back over the rocks, moving away.

35. José María Arguedas, *Obras completas* 1: 32. Subsequent page references to this story will be made parenthetically in the text.

Her eyes seemed riveted by the blade of my knife, ·they no longer looked at me but followed the blade as if magnetized. I took a step, pinning down her skirt with my foot.

(Arranqué el puñal de mi cinturón y me acerqué a ella con pasos lentos y firmes. Ella se arrastró de espaldas sobre la roca, hacia atrás. Sus ojos parecían dominados por el filo de mi cuchillo, no me miraban ya, seguían el puñal como imanados. Di un paso largo y pisé un extremo de su falda.) (37)

The reader is invited to experience the woman's "rape" vicariously by "watching" it. The complicity of the reader in the rape/murder scene is suggested by the story's structure: the narrative is in the form of a letter to a friend who is sworn to secrecy, effectively silencing the woman's dying plea for justice. The relation between the narrator and his friend (his "reader") is reproduced in that of the narrator and his rival Tomascha, whose complicity he also gains:

Yes, Tomascha, she is Satan. I'm a man, you're a man; swear to keep quiet to the death, alright?
Yes, master.

(—Sí, Tomascha, Satanás es ella. Yo hombre, tú hombre; callado como la tierra hasta tu muerte, ¿juras?
—Sí, patrón.) (34)

The last sentence of don Silvestre's letter to his friend confirms the complicity of the men in the face of the deviant woman: "Now, brother, get on your feet and swear to keep this quiet" (Ahora, hermano, ponte de pie y jura callar como la tierra, 39).

But the schema Indians-under-control / women-out-of-control is really not quite as straightforward as it seems. The possible strategy behind all this apparent male bonding in the story is to deflect attention away from the ambiguity that underlies the relation of the Indian and the "niña" (she remains nameless in the text) to the señor, and to each other. Although he tries to mask it ("I'm a man, you're a man"), Silvestre's hold over Tomascha is coercive in the same way that his hold over the woman is, and so the threat of betrayal, the threat to mastery, is equally present in the feminized Indian as in the woman.

The similarity of the Indian's position to the woman's is suggested by the curious way in which the scene of Tomascha's detailed account to don

Silvestre of the woman's seduction of him resembles the seduction scene itself. In Tomascha's account, the girl orders him into her bedroom to do something for her; once in her room, the Indian finds her sitting up in bed, one thing leads to another, and he ends up sharing it with her.

When Tomascha recounts the episode for don Silvestre, the *patrón* orders him into his room. Don Silvestre himself sits down on his bed, facing the Indian. The woman's sudden feelings of passion for Tomascha— "Tomascha!—she said to me—Tomascha! You look like a hawk . . . Truly, master, in the girl's eyes there was affection for me" (¡Tomascha!—me dijo—¡Tomascha! ¡Pareces ak'chi! . . . De verdad, patrón, en el ojo de la niña estaba el cariño para mí . . . )—echo strangely in the *señor*:

> Until that night I hadn't noticed it: Tomascha was almost beautiful, his hawklike face was energetic; he had bangs on his forehead like the untamed horses of the pampas. His sunken eyes were like those of Andean hawks, they had that expression . . .
>
> (Hasta esa noche no lo había notado: Tomascha era casi hermoso, su cara de gavilán era enérgica; tenía un cerquillo en la frente, como los potros cerriles de las pampas. Sus ojos hundidos eran casi iguales a los de los gavilanes andinos, tenían esa expresión . . . ) (34)

When Tomascha leaves, don Silvestre experiences a kind of dejection, a feeling of loss, "as if my balance had been destroyed" (como si se rompiera mi equilibrio, 35). What troubles don Silvestre is the feeling that his control over Tomascha, as over the woman, is elusive; his commanding gaze can only reach so far.

Helen Carr discusses the conflation of woman and native in the imagination of the European male:

> Woman is the European man's primary Other: using her as an image for the racial Other transfers the asymmetrical power relation embedded in her difference from the dominant patriarchal male.
>
> So man/woman, husband/wife, seducer/seduced, rapist/victim, can all be transferred to the European/non-European relationship, and the European right to mastery made natural. Secondly, by transferring this difference, all the ambivalence towards woman's unknowable otherness can also be projected on to the non-European. So the first effect of transferral is to naturalize the desire for, and legitimize the right to, possession; the second is to provide a language in which to express the fear of the Other's incalculable potential for resisting possession, and for damaging the would-be possessor.

The implication for "The Vengeful One" is clear: women and Indians are both "alarming and disturbing challenges to mastery" and must be controlled by force.[36] Tomascha's resemblance to the hawk or *ak'chi* is relevant here, for according to William Rowe, *Ak'chi* refers to "the god that for the *comuneros* is the true owner of the local land."[37] Clearly, Tomascha's threatening (and seductive) aspect is related to the suggestion of a residual mythic power that emanates from his race inscribed on his features. In the end the woman dies, and Tomascha is banished from don Silvestre's domain forever, as Kutu was from Ernesto's in "Warma Kuyay."

As in "The Vengeful One," the voyeuristic viewing of women lying abject on the ground is staged repeatedly in Arguedas's writing. An example can be seen in the persistent return of the narrator of *Deep Rivers*, Ernesto, to a scene that fascinates and repulses him in equal measure: the dark and dingy "patio interior" where the demented Marcelina—la Opa—lies prone on the ground inviting the older schoolboys to have sex with her while the younger ones look on.

La Opa is not an Indian woman; nevertheless, a series of associations with what is Indian suggests the ambiguity of her status. The narrator Ernesto frequently describes the spaces inhabited by Indians as squalid, filthy, and stinking. The *colonos*, or Indians who worked on the *haciendas*, wallow in filth: "black sweat ran down their heads onto their necks" (Un sudor negro chorreaba de sus cabezas a sus cuellos, 41; 47). A filthiness that borders on the grotesque characterizes the bars or *chicherías* where Indians and *mestizos* go to drink *chicha* and listen to music: "Huge waves of flies surged around the doorways of the *chicherías*. On the ground, a thick layer of them swarmed over the trash that was tossed out . . . Everything was black with grime and soot" (Oleadas de moscas volaban en las puertas de las chicherías. En el suelo, sobre los desperdicios que arrojaban del interior, caminaba una gruesa manta de moscas . . . Todo era negro de suciedad y de humo, 44; 51). Ernesto notices that the girl waiting on tables had a dirty face; the Indian singer "smelled of filth" (olía a suciedad).

Julio Ortega suggests that the *chichería* represents an "anti-official space," "a space of active communication," "a space of affirmation and

36. Helen Carr, "Woman/Indian: 'The American' and His Others," 49, 53.
37. William Rowe, *Mito e ideología en la obra de José María Arguedas*, 20. A *comunero* is "a member of an Indian *ayllu*, or community," as defined by Frances Horning Barraclough in *Deep Rivers*, 245.

recognition" in contrast to the oppressive atmosphere of the *colegio* (the school) and the rest of Abancay.[38] But its effect on the protagonist Ernesto, at least, seems much more ambiguous: "Many people cast inquiring glances at me . . . I felt a violent desire to go out into the street . . . My rubber shoes, my long shirt cuffs, my necktie embarrassed and upset me. I couldn't feel at home. Where to sit, and with whom? . . . I would have to leave" (Me miraban con extrañeza, muchos . . . Sentí un violento impulso por salir a la calle . . . Mis zapatos de hule, los puños largos de mi camisa, mi corbata, me cohibían, me trastornaban. No podía acomodarme. ¿Junto a quién, en dónde? . . . Debía irme, 168–70; 185–86).

Ernesto is attracted to and repulsed by the *chichería,* a symbolic space marked by the presence of (promiscuous) women, Indians, *mestizos,* and dirt. The boy describes the claustrophobic, dark *chicherías* where the clientele sit on or close to the ground as caves full of flies (46; 52). The close proximity of other bodies and the allusion to caves suggest that Ernesto's unease is related to his ambivalence about la Opa, that is, about the overpoweringly sexual aura of the place.

La Opa is also associated with dirt, pestilence, and contamination. Her face "was covered with dirt" (estaba cubierta de inmundicia, 51; 58) and the territory she inhabits, the "patio interior," doubles as a receptacle for human excrement: "several empty boxes were set up over a ditch to serve as toilets" (varios cajones huecos, clavados sobre un canal de agua, servían de excusados, 51; 58). The connection between la Opa's seductive lure and the latrine is made explicit in the schoolboy Chauca's tormented confession to Ernesto: "Why does this driveling idiot drive me crazy? . . . the latrine seizes me, with its smell, I think" (¿Por qué me aloca esta opa babienta? . . . el excusado me agarra, con su olor, creo, 83; 93). And she dies of typhus, her body overrun with the lice that spread the deadly disease. The *patio interior* and the *chichería* are dark, dank places where the trauma of sexuality is clearly associated with dirt and vermin (lice and flies). Ernesto's terror of spiders (often a symbol of female sexuality) evokes the same symbolic association (85; 95).[39]

The scatological imagery that pervades *Deep Rivers* (and Arguedas's late works *Amor mundo* [Love world, 1967] and especially *Fox from Above and*

---

38. Julio Ortega, "Texto, comunicación y cultura en *Los ríos profundos* de José María Arguedas," 64–65.

39. The spider may be a symbol of female sexuality in Western culture; in the Andean scheme of things, the *apasanka* that terrorizes Ernesto is considered a *layk'a* or *brujo* (sorcerer). *Señores e indios,* 142–46.

*Fox from Below,* where his excremental vision is at its most grotesque) can be seen in light of Mary Douglas's theories about dirt, excrement, and impurity as symbols of disorder. According to Douglas, a society's fears of instability and ultimately of dissolution are symbolically projected onto the human body, where excrescences such as sweat, blood, saliva, semen, and excrement that seep out of the body uncontrollably, as well as disease that creeps in, are seen as threats to the body's integrity and the self's ability to control its borders.[40]

The vulnerability of the State to disorder can be seen in Abancay, where the military is called in to police the borders threatened by the uncontrollable *chicheras* (women vendors of the drink *chicha*) and later by "the plague." Father Linares attempts to exorcise the disorder of contamination represented by the typhus epidemic through the use of sanitizing chemicals (*kreso*) and quarantine, while at the same time the authorities are involved in excremental warfare against the potentially contagious rebellion initiated by the *chicheras*. Excrement becomes a weapon on both sides: the rebels smear and block a bridge with a mule's intestines to provoke the status quo, as a sign to Authority that disintegration, filth, and death haunt the margins as what the forces of order repress, and the authorities retaliate by putting excrement in the women's mouths (140; 155). The scatological plays a role in class warfare in *Deep Rivers* because the Imaginary of the controlling elite has constructed an image of the oppressed Indian population as filthy, reeking, and diseased, so that the threat of revolt must inevitably be seen in terms of contagion.

Ernesto as we have noted has an ambivalent attraction to disorder (to excrement), as Arguedas does to death—the final dissolution of the body. His voyeuristic fascination for the sordid or repulsive reaches a kind of epiphanic intensity when he is drawn to the plague-infested town of Patibamba, where a grotesque scene awaits him:

> I crouched down on the ground and looked in through the crack under the door. . . . Near the hearth a girl about twelve years old was probing the body of another small girl with a long needle; . . . I looked intently and could see on the point of the needle a nest of *chigoe* larva. . . . Then I saw that the little girl's anus, her little private parts, were covered with enormous, white, insect-bitten swellings; the white sacs hung down as they did from the rear quarters of the filthiest, most abandoned hogs in that treacly valley.

40. Mary Douglas, *Purity and Danger: An Analysis of Concepts of Pollution and Taboo.*

(Miré por la rendija más próxima al piso, arrodillándome en el suelo . . . Junto al fogón de la choza, una chica como de doce años, hurgaba con una aguja larga en el cuerpo de otra niña . . . Miré fuerte, y pude ver en la punta de la aguja un nido de piques . . . Vi entonces el ano de la niña, y su sexo pequeñito, cubierto de bolsas blancas, de granos enormes de piques; las bolsas blancas colgaban como en el trasero de los chanchos, de los más asquerosos y abandonados de ese valle meloso.) (248)

In this scene the Indian girl child, whose sexual organs have been corrupted by vermin (*piques*), is associated with animality (hogs) and filth. Again, looking at the Other, sexuality and dirt converge in a single image as Ernesto surveys the diseased female body with a certain amount of erotic attraction. The intrusiveness of Ernesto's gaze here suggests the dark side of his voyeuristic will to knowledge. Later he will regard la Opa's lice-infected dying body with the same erotic charge. The burning sensation that overtakes him as he imagines the lice on la Opa crawling over his own body ("I felt as though thousands of lice were crawling over my body and heating it up" [Sentí que millares de piojos caminaban sobre mi cuerpo, y me calentaban], 209; 228), suggests the burning of desire. This obsessive surveying of the diseased female body projects the self's fear of contamination. Although the deadly typhus that threatens Abancay is clearly not syphilis, the *portero* (janitor) Abraham contracts it as a result of sexual contact with la Opa. The suggestion of syphilitic contagion is not only present with respect to la Opa, but also in the sick prostitute María of "El forastero" (The outsider) and the nymphomaniac Marcelina of *Amor mundo*.

Ernesto's personal experience of disorder and helplessness at the scene of the ravaged female body, however, is countered by the impersonal, mythic gaze of the text's ethnographic narrator (identified by Rama as "José María Arguedas the ethnologist").[41] Rama distinguishes two narrators in *Deep Rivers:* the adult Ernesto who narrates his personal experiences as an adolescent in Abancay ("The Principal Narrator"), and a narrator he calls "The Ethnologist" who narrates from the perspective of a mythic present tense, as an expert witness whose store of cultural knowledge is comparable to that of a native. Rama finds the significance of the two narrators in their transcultural counterpoint of the personal/contingent (The

41. Rama, *Transculturación narrativa,* 278.

Principal Narrator) and the mythic/eternal (The Ethnologist). It seems likely that through the anthropological perspective of the "ethnologist" Arguedas managed to transcend the disorder and unpleasure of the voyeuristic individual gaze, to ward off the disturbing psychology of the personal. The transcendence of disgust and erotic involvement in Arguedas's text is accomplished as well through the innocent bourgeois child's passionate attachment to the Indian Other's ceremony, music, and ritual. Ernesto's religious sensibility, based on the sublimating of popular practices to great spiritual heights, presumably elevates him as well to a moral level above that of his peers. Thus he claims what Stallybrass and White call "symbolic superiority" through "the accumulation of symbolic capital . . . which accrues to the sensitive soul when she or he can differentiate her/himself from the commonality by a sublime translation of popular culture into 'higher' discursive terms."[42] As for la Opa, besides her association with filth, she shares other characteristics with the Indian; her abjectness and her inarticulateness (she is mute, "demented") are like that of the servant with whom Ernesto fails to communicate at his uncle's home in Cuzco: " 'Doesn't he know how to talk?' I asked my father. 'He doesn't dare, he told me.' " (¿No sabe hablar?—le pregunté a mi padre.—No se atreve—me dijo, 14; 18). It is tempting to suggest that Arguedas displaces on to a supposedly non-Indian object (the *mestizo,* the woman) what repulses him about the Indian, a repulsion that he cannot consciously represent. El Peluca, the schoolboy most fiercely addicted to la Opa's nightly visits to the *patio interior,* openly states what the rest of the novel represses when he insults her for her inaccessibility on a night she fails to appear: "She didn't come, the Indian whore" (No ha venido, la india puta, 186; 204). Yet what repulses the narrator about la Opa, and the ambiguity of her status, might well reflect Arguedas's tormented perception of the Self as well as of the Other. For the abuse Arguedas felt he suffered as a child, the initiation into a corrupt sexuality, his supposed childhood inability to master Spanish, his conflictive identification with the Indian, led him to subliminally identify with his female characters and their silent tolerance for abuse, their inarticulateness, their abjectness, their perverse sexuality, their almost-but-not-quite Indian-ness.

There are many suggestions in *Deep Rivers* of Ernesto's kinship with la Opa. Like her, he straddles the line between Indian and non-Indian; as

---

42. Peter Stallybrass and Allon White, *The Politics and Poetics of Transgression,* 198.

his schoolmate Rondinel observes: "You're a little Indian, even though you look white! A little Indian, that's all!" (¡Eres un indiecito, aunque pareces blanco! ¡Un indiecito, no más!, 76; 85). Like la Opa, Ernesto is referred to as "demented," twice by Father Linares, and he identifies with a wandering Indian singer who strikes him also as "demented." What is la Opa then? Mute, sexually insatiable, filthy, retarded, she is a displacement of lack of control *outside* the self. Her death in a sense purifies Ernesto, liberates him from the malevolent presence of a demonic, infected twin, and leaves him free to worship the virginal queens Alcira and Salvinia.

But if la Opa is the object of the narrator's (self) disgust, she is also the vehicle for his transcendence. Toward the end of the novel, and before she contracts the disease that will kill her, la Opa asserts herself in a symbolic gesture that allows her to triumph, if only for a short time, over her oppressors. She climbs a tower and, from on high, reverses the "natural" order by usurping the power of the gaze, fixing her eyes on those below who generally looked down on her. Ernesto as usual is there to watch, having followed her in order to witness and experience vicariously her moment of transcendence on high as she "was . . . observing and inspecting the notables of Abancay. She pointed them out and passed judgment on them" (contemplaba, examinándolos, a los ilustres de Abancay. Los señalaba y enjuiciaba, 188; 207). La Opa's moment of triumph is only marred by Ernesto's intrusive presence, as he himself recognizes intuitively and abashedly: "I felt I was committing a sin watching her, a great sin that I would have to atone for" (Creía que cometía una maldad con verla. Una maldad grande que debería expiar, 189; 207). Ernesto is aware that his gaze humiliates and lessens her. Her mocking laugh at the illustrious citizens of Abancay, out of reach of their grasp, unseen and suddenly free, is a grotesque version of the folk hero doña Felipa's mocking escape from the soldiers who cannot find and jail her. But it is also perhaps a cautionary vision for the budding anthropologist, who might see in la Opa's will not to be seen a mute reproach—one that contrasts in its muteness with the blacks' more overt gesture of censure at the presence of Carpentier and Roldán at their *ñáñigo* ceremonies.

La Opa's vulnerability to the gaze of others is like Ernesto's experience as a "forastero" (outsider) in Abancay. It also suggests Arguedas's hostile reception as a *serrano* (a native of the *sierra* region) in Lima: "the first time I came to Lima I was pursued in the streets as a rare beast. They knew us as *serranos* by the way we walked and spoke" (la primera vez que vine a

Lima, fui perseguido en las calles como animal raro . . . Nos reconocían a
los 'serranos' por el modo de andar y de hablar . . . ).[43]

While being open to the gaze of others connotes weakness, what hides
itself from view, what doesn't allow itself to be seen, has a kind of
power. Demetrio tells Matilde in *All the Bloods:* "You are an *achank'aray*
flower . . . [that] grows in the midst of the snow up high. The eyes of men
can't stain it" (Eres flor achank'aray . . . Crece junto a la nieve, pues, en
lo alto. El ojo del hombre no le mancha). Nature itself derives strength
from seclusion, as does the Apurimac River that can only be seen from
the highest peaks, but whose powerful voice is heard everywhere.[44] Arguedas's association of strength or power with being hidden from view, like
his association of viewing from above with power, has a basis in Andean
tradition. Regina Harrison notes that Garcilaso "mentions Inca belief in
an invisible god, Pachacamac, one who did not allow itself to be seen
by its subjects." This same motif underlies Arguedas's conviction that the
geographic isolation of the sierra kept it strong against Spain's invasion by
slowing the advance of the alien culture.[45] It follows that the eye can be
on the one hand a vehicle for transcendent knowledge, or alternatively,
an instrument of Conquest.

Because that which remains hidden from view has this power, Arguedas
frequently associates clandestine viewing with aggression. Ernesto ap-
proaches la Opa taking great care to occult his presence, walking barefoot
and imitating the quiet gait of a cat (188; 206). Although Ernesto's persona
is that of an innocent child, his act is less than innocent. In *Canto kechwa*
(Quechua song, 1938), Arguedas recalls being told of an incident that
clearly reveals how the strategy of "ocultándose" (keeping oneself hidden)
is employed by the dominant class to certify their dominance. One night
hearing the music of a *quena* being played in a nearby hut, the hacienda
manager crept up to the door "ocultándose" and went inside, insisted
that it was the time for prayer, demanded the instrument, and crushed it
underfoot on the floor. In the same text, Arguedas associates the occulted
viewing of the Indian with sadism: in the evenings while the Indians would
fight among themselves, the hacienda manager would stand out in the hall

43. Arguedas, *Señores e indios,* 183.
44. Arguedas, *Todas las sangres,* 163; *Señores e indios,* 120.
45. Harrison, *Signs, Songs, and Memory,* 98. José María Arguedas and Francisco Izquierdo
Ríos, eds., *Mitos, leyendas y cuentos peruanos,* 14. See also Arguedas's "La sierra en el proceso
de la cultura peruana" in *Formación de una cultura nacional indoamericana,* 9–27.

and calmly look on as they went at each other throwing rocks, kicking, punching, and scratching.

These two malevolent scenes of viewing associated with hierarchy and separation contrast in the same essay with a utopistic scene of complete involvement, where everyone participates—including the *patrón*—and no one is on the outside looking in.[46] The utopia of universal participation, of a universal "we" (nosotros), is a childhood memory of plenitude for Arguedas that the adult cannot recover. The hacienda manager's behavior is that of an individual in a society diminished by the repression of Indian culture, the culture of collective involvement. The non-Indian's sadistic viewing of the Indian Other is a sign of the separation of the individual from what secretly he most desires. The gaze in Arguedas's fiction as well as his essays desires a kind of reunion with its object that by its nature is denied it, and so he becomes obsessed with the idea of distance and the perspective of the outsider.

The "master-of-all-I-survey" motif in Arguedas's fictional fantasies of control has its counterpart, then, in the association of looking with impotence, alienation, and the inability to participate fully in the activities of others. Ernesto in *Deep Rivers* divides the world into actors and spectators:

> Men swim out to the largest stones; cutting through the water they reach them and fall asleep there . . . Only the bravest swimmers, the heroes, can; the others, the faint-hearted and the children, are left behind. From the banks they watch the strongest men swim through the current . . . (24–25)

> (Los hombres nadan para alcanzar las grandes piedras, cortando el río llegan a ellas y duermen allí . . . Sólo los nadadores, los audaces, los héroes; los demás, los humildes y los niños se quedan; miran desde la orilla, cómo los fuertes nadan en la corriente . . . ) (29–30)

The anthropologist of course is a spectator looking at the Indian actors from a point outside, like the fainthearted and the children. In many of the articles Arguedas wrote about Indian rituals and ceremonies, the perspective of the outsider is foregrounded. In an essay Arguedas evokes the *waynas* or unmarried young men who, like "the heroes," brave the current rather than look on from the shore:

46. Arguedas, *Canto kechwa*, 8, 5.

Starting in the morning the young men go out into the streets playing the *flauta* . . . In groups of three to twenty walking proudly they enter the plaza from all four corners. They all play the *flauta,* as if announcing that they are free; they walk faster in the plaza, with more pride . . . looking straight ahead . . . They look through the doors of the bars at the plaza, full of young girls, like masters and leaders.

(Desde la mañana salen los waynas, los hombres solteros, a pasear en las calles, tocando flauta . . . En pandilla de tres, hasta de veinte, caminando altivos, entran a la plaza, por las cuatro esquinas. Todos tocan flauta, como anunciando que son libres; caminan más rápido en la plaza, con más orgullo . . . mirando alto . . . Salen a ratos hasta la puerta de las tiendas, y miran la plaza, llena de pasñas, como dominadores y dueños.)[47]

The young men here are clearly actors who command the narrator's respect, "walking proudly," "with pride," "free," "looking straight ahead." The *waynas* look at the young girls with a proprietary gleam, "like masters and leaders." In contrast, the narrator/anthropologist regards the young girls as an outside observer, from the periphery: "from the back" (de espaldas), "from afar" (de lejos), and his presence is an anomaly: not a single man of his class can be seen in the plaza, as they are all watching the spectacle "from the balconies of their houses" (desde los balconcitos de sus casas).[48]

The balcony is a significant image according to Peter Stallybrass and Allon White: "From the balcony, one could gaze, but not be touched." The balcony as a limit imposed on desire allows a kind of vicarious participation while inhibiting "contamination." The sensibility of the *vecino* is a modern, bourgeois one that sets the individual apart from the group:

There is no more easily recognizable scene of bourgeois pathos than the lonely crowd in which individual identity is achieved *over against* all the others, through the sad realization of not-belonging. That moment, in which the subject is made the outsider to the crowd, an onlooker, compensating for exclusion through the deployment of the discriminating gaze, is at the very root of bourgeois sensibility.[49]

47. Arguedas, *Señores e indios,* 76.
48. Arguedas, *Señores e indios,* 76–77.
49. Stallybrass and White, *The Politics and Poetics of Transgression,* 136, 187.

Those who watch the festival in Tinta from the shelter of their balconies "don't count" (No cuentan). But is their situation different from the narrator's? Does he "count"? Arguedas constructs for himself a kind of metaphorical balcony, "compensating for exclusion," for "the sad realization of not-belonging." The rhythm of the fiesta reaches a dramatic pitch that demands the full participation of its actors: "and nobody is looking because everyone is dancing" (y nadie mira, porque todos bailan).[50] Arguedas's phrase "and nobody is looking because everyone is dancing" suggests that there is no perspective outside that corresponds to the anthropologist's gaze; but clearly *someone* is watching, however much Arguedas would rhetorically occlude his alienated presence. The view from outside is, then, a conflictive stance for Arguedas. While it can indicate mastery, an assertion of control over its object, or alternatively the transcendence of the personal and its grasping, sadistic vision of control, it also reveals how the anthropologist is marginalized from the site of utopistic participation that he desires to inhabit.

In his essays, Arguedas repeatedly employs deictic markers that indicate the place on the sidelines or from afar where the anthropologist situates himself:

> I went to listen to them *from a nearby corner* . . .
> (Yo iba a escucharlos *desde una esquina próxima* . . . )
>
> *From afar, from two blocks,* you can hear the prayers . . .
> (*Desde lejos, de dos cuadras,* se oyen los rezos . . . )
>
> *At a distance*, the whole song seems only a wail . . .
> (*A distancia*, todo el canto parece sólo un alarido . . . )
>
> *From that peak* you can see in all its beauty and all its magnitude the great valley of Cajamarca.
> (*Desde esa cumbre* se ve, en toda su hermosura y en toda su magnitud, el gran valle de Cajamarca.)[51]

Here the authority derived from the subject's distance from its object represents a compensatory strategy on Arguedas's part, for elsewhere he consistently invokes the privileged authority of participation. He insists that "only he who has heard the Indians speak since childhood can discover, beyond the alphabetic signs, part of the unique phonetic richness of the

---

50. Arguedas, *Señores e indios,* 77.
51. Arguedas, *Señores e indios,* 138, 71, 86–87, 89. Emphasis added.

people's *quechua*" ([s]ólo quien ha oído desde la niñez hablar a los indios puede descubrir, detrás de los índices alfabéticos, parte de esta singular riqueza fonética del quechua popular . . . ). He invokes his authority "as a novelist who participated in his childhood in the life of Indians and *mestizos*" (como novelista que participó en la niñez de la vida de indios y mestizos . . . ). According to Arguedas, the Indian narrator (or narrators) of *Gods and Men of Huarochirí* derives authority from his status "not as an observer but as a participant" (no como observador sino como participante . . . ). The citizen of Lima, the capital of Peru, does not have the authority to represent Peruvian culture because he has experienced it "more as an observer than as a fellow countryman" (más como un observador que como un paisano).[52]

Arguedas, barred in reality from the collective involvement whose authority he claimed, more an observer than a bona fide participant in the Indians' world, found in the discourse of anthropology a way to control the alienating effects of the personal (distaste, erotic involvement, feelings of isolation). Critics who posit for Arguedas an "insider's view" based on physical and/or emotional proximity, are in danger of eliding the problematic nature of the eye in his work, and in his life.[53]

52. Arguedas, *Canciones y cuentos*, 68; *Indios, mestizos y señores*, 27; *Dioses y hombres*, 10; *Formación de una cultura*, 7.

53. According to William Rowe, Arguedas "was raised by *comuneros* during a crucial time of his childhood; this experience and the subsequent decision that his greatest loyalty would be to Quechua culture is what allowed his perception of that culture to be *that of an insider*." In *Mito e ideología*, 16. Emphasis added.

# 4 THE VOICE OF THE OTHER
Anthropological Discourse and the
*Testimonio* in *Biografía de un cimarrón*
and *Canto de sirena*

The vein of Latin American *testimonio* that uses the anthropological life history as its primary rhetorical model promotes certain myths about, its own discourse.[1] As in the life history, the central illusion fostered by the testimonial genre is that nonliterate native informants if asked will speak spontaneously and truthfully, unmediated by the rhetorical conventions that ensnare the literate writer within a literary tradition. The role of the anthropologist or the writer of a *testimonio* is to transcribe the spontaneous richness of oral narrative with a minimal amount of authorial intervention. This positioning of the writer and his or her informant is meant to guarantee that the document will be an authentic expression of the informant's voice, which the literate writer has facilitated, but not produced as such.

This rhetorical stance is clearly evident in Miguel Barnet's theoretical statements about the *testimonio,* and in his *Biografía de un cimarrón* (*Biography of a Runaway Slave*). In an essay, Barnet, quoting Alfonso Reyes, repeats the myth of the authentic native voice speaking an unmediated truth: "The voice of the dispossessed . . . is purer and more

1. Roberto González Echevarría distinguishes between the "epic" *testimonio* and the *"petite histoire,* a sort of cultural history dealing with everyday life and folk traditions." What González Echevarría calls the *"petite histoire"* is closely related to the life history in anthropology. In *The Voice of the Masters: Writing and Authority in Modern Latin American Literature,* 116. On the life history see L. L. Langness and Gelya Frank, *Lives: An Anthropological Approach to Biography.*

spontaneous because it is fresh, unrehearsed, unbound by the mantle of rhetoric." He adds that the creator of a *novela-testimonio* "should take care with this language, preserve its pristine essences, its twists and turns, its subject matter."[2]

By preserving the "pristine essences" of "the voice of the dispossessed," the *testimonio* aspires to purge itself of the literary effects that characterize previous attempts on the part of elite writers to textualize the voice of the Other. In the Cuban context, for example, the *testimonio*'s supposed authenticity is in direct contrast to caricatures of Spanish spoken by blacks in nineteenth- and twentieth-century *teatro bufo,* to what Pedro Barreda has called the "onomatopoeic primitivism" of Afro-Cuban poetry of the 1920s, and to the *costumbrista* dialogue of blacks in nativist works such as Carpentier's *¡Ecué-yamba-O!*[3]

Critics have noted that the intention of the *testimonio* is to divest itself— or to appear to divest itself—of the effects of the literary. According to John Beverley the *testimonio,* in contrast to the novel, is "primarily concerned with sincerity, rather than literariness." Renato Prada Oropeza cites as one of the characteristic traits of testimonial discourse a concern with truth rather than beauty, marked by the absence of literary devices or aesthetic pretensions common to literary genres such as the short story and the novel.[4]

The Peruvian writer Gregorio Martínez calls his *Canto de sirena* (Siren's song, 1977) a "novela-testimonio," adopting the same term Barnet uses to refer to *Biography of a Runaway Slave.*[5] But although he situates his text within the generic bounds of *testimonio,* Martínez subverts the conventions of the testimonial genre by continually foregrounding its literariness, and by problematizing the relation of the marginal voice of the black protagonist Candelario Navarro to elite discourses. While Barnet's statements about the *testimonio* and the mystifications of the text itself produce a rhetoric of authenticity that turns out to be an illusion, in *Siren's Song* Martínez exposes the fundamental duplicity of the rhetorical positions taken by Barnet and others in a self-consciously parodic version of the genre.

2. Miguel Barnet, "Testimonio y comunicación: una vía hacia la identidad," 51.

3. For a critical reading of this history see Pedro Barreda, *The Black Protagonist in the Cuban Novel.*

4. John Beverley, "The Margin at the Center: On *Testimonio* (Testimonial Narrative)," 15; Renato Prada Oropeza, "De lo testimonial al testimonio: Notas para un deslinde del discurso-testimonio," 13.

5. Cited in Luis Fernando Vidal, "Review of *Canto de sirena,*" 164.

## I. Primitivism and the Native Voice in Barnet's *Biography of a Runaway Slave*

Barnet takes great pains to suggest that he functions in *Biography of a Runaway Slave* merely as the transparent medium through which the native voice expresses itself spontaneously. He speaks of "the suppression of the I" as being indispensable in producing a testimonial novel and describes the writing process in terms of possession; the Other possesses his mind and body and essentially speaks through him: "I couldn't sleep . . . I was in a state of complete insomnia, because I had become the character . . . And then the time comes when you find yourself in the hills talking with the trees. . . . Do you understand? You are an other."[6]

The voice of Esteban here is described as a spontaneous flow that Barnet mediates but doesn't actually produce. This myth is related to Miguel Angel Asturias's characterization of himself as "el Gran Lengua" (the Great Tongue) through whom the ancient voice of the Maya reemerges to speak again in the present.[7] The same myth is taken up by the anthropologist Elisabeth Burgos-Debray in her introduction to *Me llamo Rigoberta Menchú,* where she describes her role with respect to her informant in these terms: "I became . . . her instrument, her double by allowing her to make the transition from the spoken to the written word."[8] Significantly, Burgos-Debray uses quotations from Asturias's 1949 novel *Hombres de maíz* (*Men of Maize*) as epigraphs to several chapters in Menchú's *testimonio,* underscoring the dependence of the native voice on the anthropologist/scribe as medium.

The voice of the Other has for Barnet and for Burgos-Debray a redemptive function, as their identification of Self with the Other becomes a journey back to a lost wholeness. Burgos-Debray says of Rigoberta Menchú: "As we listen to her voice, we have to look deep into our own

6. Barnet speaks of the suppression of the "I" in "La novela testimonio," 23. The quote is cited in Bejel, "Entrevista," 49. Barnet's transformation into Montejo in the process of writing recalls Flaubert's professed self-transformations into Mme. Bovary, Bouvard and Pécuchet, and into a cannibal for the writing of *Salammbô*. See C. J. Rawson, "Cannibalism and Fiction: Reflections on Narrative Form and 'Extreme' Situations." Rawson notes that it was the Romantics who first valued "the artist as a Protean impersonator," 684.

7. See Carlos Rincón, "Nociones surrealistas, concepción del lenguaje y función ideológico-literaria del realismo mágico en Miguel Angel Asturias," 40.

8. Elisabeth Burgos-Debray, ed., *I . . . Rigoberta Menchú: An Indian Woman in Guatemala,* translated by Ann Wright, xx. This is a translation of Burgos-Debray's *Me llamo Rigoberta Menchú y así me nació la conciencia,* 18.

souls for it awakens sensations and feelings which we, caught up as we are in an inhuman and artificial world, thought were lost forever." Rigoberta, Burgos-Debray says, "allowed me to discover another self. Thanks to her, my American self is no longer something 'uncanny.' "[9]

Barnet similarly attributes redemptive power to the Other's voice: "The conceptual richness, the multi-faceted quality of oral expression, the cosmogony of the Cuban man, have allowed me to approach that Mecca so desired by all: an identity." Barnet has described his experience of the Cuban Revolution as one of rebirth, as the discovery of the richness of Cuba's history and folklore, and taking up ethnography became for the writer "a recuperation of my self."[10]

According to Christopher Herbert, the theme of rebirth is a recurring "mythic narrative" in anthropology. The anthropologist undergoes the traumatic experience of fieldwork, during which he must in a sense abandon or detach himself from his own culture, sacrifice or repress the Self in order to open himself fully to the Other. In Barnet's case, the testimonial novel will be an expression of his newfound national and personal authenticity and a repudiation of the inauthentic influence of North American imperialism on Cuban culture.[11]

The fetishization of the native voice that underlies Barnet's and Burgos-Debray's statements on the *testimonio* goes back to early modern conceptions about the language of primitive man. Rousseau claimed that the first utterances of man were poetic, metaphoric rather than analytical. In his view, the primitive impulse to speak is spontaneous, innocent, and devoid of the artificiality of rational thought; the metaphorical language of the savage expresses passion rather than abstract concepts. In *The Fall of Natural Man,* Anthony Pagden discusses European perceptions of native speech in the New World. He notes that for Charles de Brosses, Rousseau's contemporary, "the languages of 'savages' were rich in metaphor precisely because such people were more dependent on 'passion' than 'reason.' " Pagden cites as well the Mexican Ortiz de Hinojosa, who claimed that Indian languages " 'are so inaccessible and difficult that they do not seem

---

9. Burgos-Debray, ed., *I . . . Rigoberta Menchú,* xii, xxi. *Me llamo Rigoberta Menchú,* 10, 18.

10. Barnet, *La fuente viva,* 5; cited in Bejel, "Entrevista," 45–46.

11. Christopher Herbert, *Culture and Anomie: Ethnographic Imagination in the Nineteenth Century,* especially chapter 3. See Barnet's essay "Testimonio y comunicación." Roberto González Echevarría discusses the theme of conversion in post-Revolutionary Cuban literature and as a recurring topos of literary modernity in *Voice of the Masters,* 110–23.

to have been created by men, but by nature, with the illiterate voices of birds and brute animals, which could not be written down in any kind of script.'" Pagden notes that "in Hinojosa's opinion you could no more transcribe an Indian word than you could the cry of a baboon."[12]

The voice of the Other continues to ravish modern writers with its poetic, spontaneous, antirational, seductive art. One thinks of the beautiful, wild creature Rima, whose birdlike voice seduces Abel before he ever lays eyes on her in William Henry Hudson's *Green Mansions.* More recently, Eduardo Galeano presents the language of native Americans as richly metaphoric:

> The Guarau Indians, who live on the outskirts of the Earthly Paradise, call the rainbow *serpent of necklaces* and the firmament *the sea above.* Lightning is *the brightness of rain.* The friend, *my other heart.* The soul, *the breast's sun.* The owl, *master of the dark night.* To say "cane," they say *continual grandson* and to say "forgiveness," they say *forgetting.*[13]

Esteban Montejo, according to Barnet, "imitates the sound of birds, the movement of leaves." Montejo's voice is an expression of nature; according to Barnet, in *Biography of a Runaway Slave* "a dialogue develops that is already part of a completely magical hierarchy: between the trees and Esteban, between the birds and Esteban."[14] Indeed, Barnet presents Montejo as a genuine primitive, of nature and in thrall to nature. As a runaway slave who hides out in a cave avoiding contact with his fellow men, scavenging for food, leading a rudimentary, essentially nomadic existence and deriving all his needs from nature, Montejo can be compared to the archetypal Wild Man of legend. According to Stephen Greenblatt, "[w]ild Men live beyond the pale of civilized life, outside all institutions, untouched by the long, slow development of human culture. If their existence is rude and repugnant, it also has . . . a disturbing allure."[15] From the beginning, Montejo speaks as primitive man in awe of nature and its inexplicable manifestations:

> There are things in life I do not understand. Everything about Nature seems obscure to me, and the gods even more.

12. Anthony Pagden, *The Fall of Natural Man: The American Indian and the Origins of Comparative Ethnology,* 184, 183.

13. Eduardo Galeano, *Memoria del fuego,* 62.

14. Cited in Bejel, "Entrevista," 42, 41–42.

15. Stephen Greenblatt, "Learning to Curse: Aspects of Linguistic Colonialism in the Sixteenth Century," 566–67.

(Hay cosas que yo no me explico de la vida. Todo eso que tiene que ver con la Naturaleza para mí está muy oscuro, y lo de los dioses más.)[16]

These first lines of the text set the tone for the primitivism that pervades Barnet's novel.[17] Montejo's monologue repeats well-worn stereotypes of primitive man: the primitive has an intimate relation to nature and is awed by natural phenomena; the primitive has a childlike, receptive mind that is not analytical; the primitive is an ingenuous innocent driven by childlike impulses; the primitive thinks in terms of myth or legend rather than history; the primitive is superstitious and irrational. In the opening paragraph Montejo recounts his experience of an eclipse as one of awe before a veritable cataclysm: "Some died of heart attacks, and some were struck dumb" (Hubo quien se murió del corazón y quien se quedó mudo, 17; 23).

This naive rapture before the phenomena of the natural world represents the tension between Barnet's science and Montejo's primitive superstition that underlies the narrative. The eclipse as invoked by Montejo refers back to the primal scene described by López de Gómara in which the native Other confronts the power of the West to claim mastery, using scientific knowledge to subjugate the superstitious primitive:

[T]hey didn't want to give food to Columbus's men, rather they plotted to kill them. Columbus then called to some of them, chastizing them for their lack of charity . . . and threatened that if they didn't sell them food, they would all die of a plague; and to prove his power he told them that on a certain day they would see the moon turn blood red. When they saw the eclipse they believed what Columbus said since they were ignorant of astrology. They cried and begged Columbus's pardon and brought him everything he asked for.[18]

16. Miguel Barnet, *Biography of a Runaway Slave,* 17; *Biografía de un cimarrón,* 23. Subsequent page references within the text will refer first to the translation and then to the original.

17. Barnet's primitivism has not been addressed by critics; instead, many have focused on his stated goal of rewriting history from below and its implications. From this perspective see William Luis, "The Politics of Memory and Miguel Barnet's *The Autobiography of a Runaway Slave*" and Antonio Vera-León, "Montejo, Barnet, el cimarronaje y la escritura de la historia." See also Elzbieta Sklodowska, *"Biografía de un cimarrón* de Miguel Barnet: revisión de la historia afrocubana."

18. Francisco López de Gómara, *Historia general de las Indias,* vols. 1–2: 62.

Consciously or unconsciously, by restaging this scene, Barnet inscribes his text in the history of Western domination that anthropology repeats. Directly following his reminiscences about the eclipse, Montejo narrates his version of the beginnings of slavery—another tale of mastery and submission:

> In my opinion it all began with the red kerchiefs. . . . the blacks, excited by the red, ran like little lambs to the boats, and they were caught right there. Black men have always really liked red. That color is to blame for putting chains on them and sending them to Cuba. (18)

> (Para mí que todo empezó cuando los pañuelos *punzó*. . . . los negros, embullados con el punzó, corrían como ovejitas para los barcos y ahí mismo los cogían. Al negro siempre le ha gustado mucho el punzó. Por culpa de ese color les pusieron las cadenas y los mandaron para Cuba.) (24)

Here the childlike, sensual impulses of the blacks condemn them to be enslaved by their natural masters. The blacks' historical fate, like that of the Indians in the Ur-story about the eclipse, is to be seduced and betrayed by enterprising Europeans who are able to exploit primitive impulses for their own ends. Again, there is an echo here of the relationship between anthropologist and informant as a kind of seductive coercion. Rather than red kerchiefs, however, Barnet supplied Montejo with "tobacco, trinkets, photographs, etcetera" (tabacos, distintivos, fotografías, etcétera, 16).[19]

The conflict between a desire to be seduced by the primitive and a desire to impose mastery goes back to the beginnings of ethnography as a discipline. Ethnographers sought to master the native by applying ethnographic categories and collecting, but were secretly in thrall to the Other's "primitive" ways. These contradictions at the heart of the discipline are played out in *Biography of a Runaway Slave*.[20]

On many occasions Barnet claims the prestige of science for his text. To produce a *testimonio,* he says, sound scientific knowledge of the period is crucial. In the introduction to *Biography of a Runaway Slave,* he describes the novel as a product of standard ethnographic research and reliance

19. Barnet's introduction, from which this quote is drawn, does not appear in Hill's translation.

20. According to Susan Sontag, "[m]odern sensibility moves between two seemingly contradictory but actually related impulses: surrender to the exotic, the strange, the other; and the domestication of the exotic, chiefly through science." In "The Anthropologist as Hero," 185.

on precise historical data. He considers the *testimonio* to be a document offering fruitful material for sociological and historical analyses, and calls his informant a "laboratory."[21] Barnet invokes science as the privileged discourse of Revolutionary consciousness in Cuba in opposition to the frivolousness of pre-Revolutionary bourgeois self-consciousness. He favors a "depersonalization . . . in which art approximates science." The appropriation of popular culture as the basis for an authentic national identity needs to be carried out using the tools of science, not improvisation.[22]

The footnotes and glossary Barnet includes in the novel give it the aura of a scientific document. The glossary ostensibly serves to explicate expressions that would otherwise be incomprehensible to the reader; but in most cases in which a word spoken by Montejo is glossed in the text, the definition merely repeats what the informant has already explained:

> After some time had passed, and the [*esquifación,* which was the] slaves' clothing was worn out, they would give the men a new set made of Russian cloth or canvas. (25)

> (Cuando pasaba algún tiempo y la *esquifación,* que era la ropa de los esclavos, se gastaba, le daban a los hombres una nueva a base de tela de rusia.) (32)

> I didn't start whistling again because the guajiros or the slave catchers could come. Since the cimarrón was a slave who had escaped, the masters sent a posse of rancheadores after them. Mean guajiros with hunting dogs so they could drag you out of the woods in their jaws. (47)

> (Y no volví a chiflar, porque podían venir los guajiros o los *ranchadores.* Como el cimarrón era un esclavo que se huía, los amos mandaban a una cuadrilla de ranchadores; guajiros brutos con perros de caza, para que lo sacaran a uno del monte a mordiscos.) (56)[23]

Similarly, Barnet's footnotes are seemingly added with no other purpose than that of authorizing what Montejo has already said. Only the

---

21. Barnet, "La novela testimonio," 38; "Testimonio y comunicación," 51.

22. Barnet, "Testimonio y comunicación," 48; "La novela testimonio," 48. The "depersonalization" and the revolutionary, scientific purity of form that Barnet calls for coincide with literary modernism's predilection for impersonal, distilled forms of life in art. In fact, Barnet's "depersonalization . . . in which art approximates science" is a quote from T. S. Eliot. Flaubert also felt that the writer should employ the dispassionate, clinical eye of the scientist; see Barnet's "La novela testimonio," where he invokes Flaubert, Eliot, and Woolf as models together with the anthropologists Malinowsky, Ortiz, and Nina Rodríguez.

23. See also for example *jila,* 31; *enkangues,* 35; *vendutas,* 35.

anthropologist, apparently, can authorize the Other's words through his interventions. Thus Barnet's text repeats positivistic claims of the superiority of Reason over the irrational Other, even as he invokes the "romantic myth of popular communion," by distancing his own discourse of reason from that of Montejo's, presented "as a site deprived of rational discourse."[24]

Without intervention, Barnet found, Montejo's mode of narration was digressive and he was prone to "fantasías." As he tends to wander, the irrational Other has to be harnessed, made to walk a (discursive) straight line: "it's a mistake to let the informant follow the rhythm of his digressions . . . you have to *lead him* a little, *force him* in a direction . . . you have to present him with pre-formulated questions."[25] This strategy of entrapment and coercion allows Barnet to constitute Montejo's life in terms of the ethnographic categories that inform his questionnaires. Just as Bernardino Sahagún in order to extract information from his informants in the sixteenth century uses questionnaires which, according to Todorov, "impose a European organization on American knowledge," Barnet's "pre-formulated" categories insinuate a hidden structure into Montejo's narrative. Ethnographic categories translate what the European experiences as exotic in the Other's cultural and geographical milieu: eating habits, cooking practices, specialized knowledge such as curing and sorcery, festival time, sexual practices, flora, fauna, superstition. In documenting the extent to which these categories have *produced* certain patterns through which knowledge of the Other is predetermined, it is worth noting that Todorov experiences the absence of discussions of sexual practices in Sahagún's *Historia general de las cosas de la Nueva España* as an inexplicable exclusion: "we learn very little," he complains, "concerning the Aztecs' sexual life from Sahagún's book."[26]

Barnet, like Todorov, displays anthropology's perennial, prurient interest in "the sexual life of savages." Montejo seduces Barnet with what he can reveal about "sexual life in the slaves' barracoons" and "the celibate man's

---

24. According to Neil Larsen, the presumed transcendence of the conflict between civilized reason and barbarous unreason in neoregionalist writers like Arguedas and Rulfo is an illusion created by the simulation of unmediated popular speech in these writers. The voice of reason, Larsen argues, has been displaced rather than subverted, "has now learned to represent itself exclusively in the cultural/aesthetic signs of its Other." In *Modernism and Hegemony: A Materialist Critique of Aesthetic Agencies,* 62.

25. Barnet, "La novela testimonio," 37. Emphasis added.

26. Tzvetan Todorov, *The Conquest of America: The Question of the Other,* 233.

encounter with nature."[27] The detached scientist steps aside to reveal the erotically involved artist. Barnet's myth of scientific detachment set against his mythic tale of fusion with the Other in the process of writing suggests a conflict between the desire for mastery and a desire for submission. Montejo's folk wisdom, his knowledge of specialized practices like curing, midwifery, and cooking along with its specialized vocabulary (*ítamorreal, harina amalá, yonyó, chequeté*) is appropriated by Barnet's science, brought under the control of its domain, translated into the written code of ethnography. Montejo's knowledge becomes a generalized knowledge for Western consumption.

Anthropology makes these "scriptural conquests," says Michel de Certeau, in order to constitute its own discursive space by transferring the "unenlightened" practices of popular cultures and primitive societies into the realm of enlightened knowledge: "there corresponds to the constitution of a scientific space, as the precondition of any analysis, the necessity of being able to *transfer* the objects of study into it."[28] If Montejo needs the authorization of science in order to speak, conversely Barnet's science needs Montejo's "wildness" in order to have anything to say.

Nevertheless, Barnet is inexorably drawn to and insistently returns to the place where Montejo's narrative betrays the limits of scientific mastery. Montejo's belief in the supernatural phenomena and irrational superstitions he describes confirms Barnet's positional superiority in relation to his informant's primitive otherness; but the irrational exerts a seductive power over the scientific imagination as a return of what science represses and excludes from its domain. Montejo in a matter-of-fact manner speaks of witches who would fly from the Canary Islands to Cuba (117; 126), of blacks "flying" to Africa (120; 129), of mermaids who entertained men underwater (117; 125–26), of meeting up with ghosts (116; 125) and headless horsemen (117; 126), and of encounters with the devil (124; 133). He claims to have seen old black men who turned into animals (128; 137) and a rooster that came back to life after having been eaten (131; 140).

Michel de Certeau suggests that superstition "puts into question the 'reason' behind power and knowledge hierarchies."[29] The original confrontation between the West and the natives of the New World took place

27. Cited in Bejel, "Entrevista," 41. On the erotic desires underlying primitivism see Marianna Torgovnick, *Gone Primitive: Savage Intellects, Modern Lives.*

28. Michel de Certeau, *The Practice of Everyday Life,* 20.

29. Certeau, *The Practice of Everyday Life,* 20.

at a time when such hierarchies were firmly established and not open to question. From the sixteenth-century chronicles to the travel writings of the nineteenth century, the Other's superstitions were frequently invoked in order to be mastered rhetorically in the space of the text.

The superstitious natives in Fray Toribio de Motolinía's account "believed in a thousand omens and signs and had a great many superstitions regarding the owl, and if they heard him screech or howl while sitting on top of a house they said that soon someone from that house would die." The Indians stubbornly persisted in their irrational beliefs even after becoming good Christians (in Motolinía's view) because of the "spells and illusions with which the devil deceived them."[30] López de Gómara lamented the deluded state in which the Indians lived, as they believed the sun and moon emerged from a cave and the first man and woman from another. "It would take a long time to recount all their superstitions," he remarks.[31]

Jean de Léry complained that the Tupinamba, when they hear a screech-owl,

> have the fantasy printed in their brain that their deceased relatives and friends are sending them these birds as a sign of good luck, and especially to encourage them to bear themselves valiantly in war against their enemies. They believe firmly that if they observe what is signified to them by these augurs, not only will they vanquish their enemies in this world, but what is more, when they die their souls will not fail to rejoin their ancestors behind the mountains and dance with them.[32]

In the nineteenth century, Everard F. im Thurn in *Among the Indians of Guiana* demonstrates how little the natives' experience of the natural world corresponds to reality: "they had heard an *omar* (an evil being) and . . . were looking for it, but, as the tracks showed in the morning, the noise had been made by a poor little labba (Coelogenys paca)." The Guiana Indian, says im Thurn, before going out to hunt "has planted various sorts of 'beenas' or plants, generally caladiums, which he supposes to act as charms to make the capture of game certain."[33]

30. Fray Toribio de Motolinía, *Historia de la Nueva España*, 256–58.
31. López de Gómara, *Historia general de las Indias*, 66.
32. De Léry, *History of a Voyage to the Land of Brasil*, 91.
33. Everard F. im Thurn, *Among the Indians of Guiana*, 19, 228.

These types of phrases—"he supposes to," "they believe firmly [i.e. wrongly] that . . ."—are deployed by Léry, im Thurn, and others to establish rhetorically the West's mastery over the wrongheaded, simpleminded natives. In *Biography of a Runaway Slave* the specific rhetorical strategies for asserting mastery have changed, but not the necessity of some strategy by which the native is subjugated and his ingenuous view of the world exposed through writing. Although Barnet doesn't explicitly refute Montejo's beliefs, the reader finds them jarring and unacceptable, as he does Mackandal's alleged escape in Carpentier's *The Kingdom of This World*. The reader by virtue of being a literate Westerner and consumer of ethnographic texts about the Other finds confirmation in Montejo's irrational superstitions and claims of his exotic primitive Otherness, while at the same time Barnet finds confirmation of his privileged position as an anthropologist.[34]

What starts out in *Biography of a Runaway Slave* as primitive babble, however, progresses toward revolutionary consciousness in a move that involves what Stephen Tyler has called "an explicit, but unacknowledged, convention" of ethnographic studies. According to Tyler, the way in which chapters are ordered in an ethnography reflects "the trope of perfective movement of spirit or intelligence from the natural to the supernatural, from the gross, material aspects of the world to those of spiritual or aesthetic understanding which has informed the whole of theological, philosophical, and scientific discourse in the West." An ethnography might begin, for example, with "material culture," "economic organization," "kinship and social structure," and end with "religion and ritual," or "art and dance," so that for Tyler, "[t]he order of chapters in a typical ethnographic study recapitulates the evolution of man from nature to culture."[35] In Barnet's novel, the Revolution becomes the implicit end point of an evolutionary climb from childlike ignorance and slavery to self-consciousness and liberation. The black's conversion from natural man to revolutionary is accomplished by the end when Montejo has become an actor in history rather than a passive dupe of the white man's strategic sorcery.

But the insistent appeal of the supernatural in Montejo's narrative to which Barnet returns again and again suggests a kind of symmetry or

---

34. In this regard, see Vincent Crapanzano's confession about the demoness who plagues his informant Tuhami: "For me, of course, 'A'isha Qandisha represented the confrontation with the exotic, the bizarre, and the mad. She attested to my identity as an anthropologist and to my doing fieldwork." In *Tuhami: Portrait of a Moroccan,* 15.

35. Stephen A. Tyler, "Ethnography, Intertextuality, and the End of Description," 87.

standoff between informant and anthropologist: if the primitive mind is seduced by the marvelous, so is the author's. The chroniclers were seemingly
unaware of the contradiction between their own superstitious fantasies
about the New World (the belief that Amazons, *El Dorado,* and mermaids
existed) and their unmitigated contempt for native superstitions that certainly weren't any more fantastic or unprovable. Critics have noted that for
the explorers of the New World from Columbus on, the native was a tabula
rasa on which the European might inscribe what he would—a perception
aptly stated by im Thurn: "The Indian mind is like a highly polished mirror
which reflects all that is shown it."[36] In *Biography of a Runaway Slave*
the reciprocal nature of this process is established by Montejo's repeated
allusions to whites appropriating for themselves, being seduced by, the
"primitive" customs and beliefs of their black Others:

> The ñáñigos fought among themselves in that African way . . . You
> can't say they were savages because the whites who got involved with
> the ñáñigo movement also practiced that custom. (154)

> (los ñáñigos se fajaban entre sí con la costumbre africana . . . y no se
> puede decir que eran salvajes, porque esa costumbre la seguían los
> blancos también, los que se metieron en el ñañiguismo.) (163)

> The game of mayombe was linked to religion. Even the overseers got
> involved, hoping to benefit. They believed in ghosts so that's why
> nobody today should be surprised that whites also believe in those
> things. (27)

> (El juego de mayombe estaba amarrado a la religión. Hasta los propios
> mayores se metían para buscarse sus beneficios. Ellos creían en los
> brujos, por eso nadie se puede asombrar de que los blancos crean en
> estas cosas.) (34)[37]

Through these observations by Montejo, the text alludes to the compelling logic of its own construction and situates Barnet and Montejo in an
ongoing history of mutual seduction and appropriation between the West
and its Others that began with the Conquest and the process of colonization
it set in motion.[38]

36. Im Thurn, *Among the Indians of Guiana,* 372.
37. See also pages 32, 85, 139.
38. On the dynamics of what he calls "mimetic appropriation" see Stephen Greenblatt,
*Marvelous Possessions: The Wonder of the New World.*

Despite what Barnet intends for *Biography of a Runaway Slave,* then, underlying Esteban Montejo's narrative are the stories it tells about its own construction: about the conflict between Barnet's science and his primitivism; about the anthropological vocation as an experience of conversion; about the evolution from primitive babble to revolutionary consciousness; and about the erotic involvement of the Self with the seductions of the Other's voice.

## II. Intertextuality, Parody, and the *Testimonio* in Gregorio Martínez's *Siren's Song*

Linda Hutcheon defines parody as "inscribing continuity while permitting critical distance," working within a certain convention or code while questioning its conventionality at the same time.[39] In *Siren's Song,* Gregorio Martínez both writes a *testimonio* and writes against it; throughout the novel literary allusions and devices, the use of shifting rhetorical registers, quotation, parody, and a self-reflexivity that implicates the informant as well as the writer undermine the presentation of Candelario Navarro's voice as spontaneous, unmediated expression.

One reason that the *testimonio* has not in general been the object of parody is the genuine admiration we feel for an exemplary or heroic protagonist whose struggles and victories against oppression are real and affecting. There is, however, perhaps deliberately, nothing exemplary or representative about Candelario Navarro. Unlike Esteban Montejo in *Biography of a Runaway Slave,* a witness and protagonist of dramatic historical changes whose voice Barnet engages in a "sacred mission" to rewrite history from below, Candelario lives a life of mesmerizing stasis in a desolate region of coastal Peru—the region centered in Nazca to which Martínez returns in all his writings.[40] Candelario is a compulsive wanderer; his wanderings trace a circular, regressive path back to his origins in Coyungo where he remains outside of history, motivated by eros as when he first leaves Coyungo "in 1914, that year when there was a war and I took off after a woman . . ." (ese año de la guerra cuando me fui siguiendo a una mujer . . . ).[41]

39. Linda Hutcheon, *A Theory of Parody: The Teachings of Twentieth-Century Art Forms,* 20.
40. Martínez has received almost no critical attention. His works include *Tierra de caléndula* (1975); *Canto de sirena* (1977); *La gloria del piturrín y otros embrujos de amor* (1985) and *Crónica de músicos y diablos* (1991).
41. Gregorio Martínez, *Canto de sirena,* 16. Subsequent page references to this work will be made parenthetically in the text.

John Beverley suggests that "[t]he narrator in *testimonio* . . . speaks for, or in the name of, a community or group, approximating in this way the symbolic function of the epic hero." Candelario, however, speaks not for his people but rather as an irremediably excentric individual, doubly marginalized as a black man in a country whose culture is defined by the transculturation between the European and the indigenous.[42]

Both Elena Poniatowska and Miguel Barnet have spoken and written at length about the nature of their relationship with their informants "Jesusa Palancares" and Esteban Montejo, and the specific circumstances in which their *testimonios* were produced. By thus invoking Jesusa's and Esteban's existence outside the text, they emphasize their status as real human beings rather than as literary creations. Martínez has not adopted this strategy, has offered no anecdotes about his relationship with Candelario or about the interview process. The absence of this convention of testimonial discourse reinforces the textual, literary nature of his novel, and leaves the reader uncertain whether Candelario exists as a real informant or, quite possibly, as a creature of the author's imagination.

The title *Siren's Song* suggests that what one critic calls "the poetic charm inherent in popular language" is a siren's song that seduces and entraps the reader.[43] A fundamental aspect of Barnet's project in *Biography of a Runaway Slave* was to recreate the spontaneous freshness, originality, and creative expressiveness of his informant's speech: the proverbs, the folk wisdom, the popular slang, the exotic words, the rhythm. Like Barnet, Martínez is drawn to the "charm" of popular speech as an alternative aesthetic. At the same time, however, Martínez is aware that his attraction to the Other's speech implies a certain voyeurism:

> [T]he novel is a siren's song for the bourgeoisie who always tend to appropriate popular art when they see it has value; they quickly domesticate or exalt it or make it their own, capture it (what I'm allowing to happen perhaps with the kind of exoticism the book contains.)[44]

The susceptibility of elite writers like Martínez to the erotic lure of the siren's song is reflected in the novel's persistent return to the theme of

---

42. Beverley, "The Margin at the Center," 16. Jean Franco, in *Plotting Women: Gender and Representation in Mexico,* 178, observes that the same excentric marginality that distinguishes Candelario also characterizes Jesusa Palancares in Elena Poniatowska's *Hasta no verte Jesús mío.*

43. Sklodowska, *"Biografía de un cimarrón* de Miguel Barnet," 47.

44. Cited in Vidal, "Review of *Canto de sirena,*" 166.

seduction. Candelario himself is obsessed by the ruses of seduction; he describes his basic strategy at the very beginning of the novel: "to give her confidence I gave her flowers and offered to marry her, and I would put in her hand a pretty present with some poetry and whatever lie it would take to sweeten her up" (para darle confianza le ofrecía flores y casarme con ella, toma, y le ponía en la mano un obsequio bien pintadito, con un verso y cualquier otra mentira que sirviera para endulzarla, 17). His exaggerated sexual fantasies insist on calling attention to the position of the reader (and implicitly that of the author) as voyeur, as complicit in the constitution of the black as an exotic Other and as a primitive sexual being.

The figure of the reader as voyeur appears in the text as a third party to whom Candelario relates in great detail his encounters with Marcela Denegri at the river where she would go to bathe: "when I got back from the river . . . he would be waiting for me anxiously" (cuando yo regresaba del río . . . él ya estaba esperándome ansioso, 99). This avid consumer of Candelario's seductive narrative powers is both a figure for the reader of Martínez's novel as a consumer of popular culture and for its author. Like him, many people come to Candelario for his knowledge of a wide range of specialized practices, including prayers to make women fall in love and a cure that involves boiling snakes. According to Candelario, he can cure cattle of worm infestation and he also claims to have a way of keeping fish fresh indefinitely.

Candelario's involved descriptions of idiosyncratic cultural practices—he goes on about castrating bulls, for example, for three pages—is a kind of parodic imitation of ethnographic discourse. For the ethnographer, the accumulation of data from informants implies that members of a culture possess a shared repertory of knowledge that confirms their collective sense of identity. The presumption of the life history is that an individual member of a culture will represent and articulate the ethos of the group as a whole. But Candelario's radical marginality makes this problematic. His knowledge is that of an isolated individual who has lost all but the formulae, the skeletal remains of a collective tradition: an *oración* (prayer) here, a *remedio* (cure) there. The absence of such a tradition to anchor the individual can be seen in Candelario's lament for a cousin who takes her specialized knowledge of how to castrate pigs to the grave without having passed it along (130).

Candelario's concern for the preservation of certain esoteric arts is an expression of the desire to salvage the cultural practices of a tradi-tional society threatened by the effects of modernization that underlies the anthropological life history, the ethnography, and the *testimonio*. His own various and excentric arts give Candelario the reputation of a sorcerer, and he has a market for his products among white consumers, who come by while he is preparing his snake remedy.

Martínez situates this consumption of popular culture by the dominant classes in the history of exploitation of Indian culture in Peru. The first words of the novel contained in an epigraph are those of Antonio Raimondi, an Italian naturalist who wrote extensively of his travels and studies in Peru in the nineteenth century. Raimondi's writings document the collecting, naming, and cataloguing of flora and fauna, as well as the scavenging of Indian tombs or *huacas* that took place in the nineteenth century in the name of science. Through his "escavaciones" the scientist appropriates the cultural patrimony of the Other, arranges it, catalogues it, writes about it, and lodges it in a museum of natural history or of antiquities.

Martínez's use of a passage from Raimondi is not casual, for among Candelario's various occupations is that of *huaquero*. "Huaquería" ("Wakería") as defined by Julio C. Tello, a prominent Peruvian archaeologist for whom Candelario claims to have worked, "consists of finding and digging up tombs in order to remove from them the offerings that accompany the dead, principally pieces of pottery or *wakos*."[45]

Candelario has a lot to say about the fine art of *huaquería* throughout the novel, and much of it bears a striking resemblance to Tello's words on the subject. In his writings, Tello extols the noble aims of archaeology as a fine art and specialized science dedicated to the study and preservation of an important cultural and historical patrimony, while denouncing the ignoble and ongoing exploitation of Indian antiquities for profit that began with the Conquest. He distinguishes the educated and skillful archaeologist from the ignorant vandals motivated by profit:

> Archaeology is a specialized science like Medicine or Engineering, and requires technical expertise . . . The archaeologist should have experience in order to observe, register and value properly whatever turns up in the excavation process . . . The modern-day search for buried treasure is a diversion or sport like hunting . . . The treasure hunter is generally indifferent to historical or artistic concerns.[46]

45. Julio C. Tello, *Páginas Escogidas,* 191.
46. Tello, *Páginas Escogidas,* 187–90.

Candelario conceives of his vocation in terms of Tello's high standards, and in his narrative one can detect a dialogic encounter with the Peruvian archaeologist's words and concerns:

> There are practically no experienced *huaqueros* left, all anyone cares about is fine pottery, cloth and gold . . . those who come driving around buying and taking everything away to Lima or out of the country have brought only ruin, ambition and desecration . . .
>
> (casi ya no queda huaquero de experiencia, de estudio, todo es la ambición por el huaco bonito, el tejido fino, el oro . . . los que vienen comprando en carro y con bastantes billetes para llevárselo todo a Lima, al extranjero, esos han metido aquí el estropeo, la profanación, la ambicia . . . ) (32)

Candelario's appropriation of Tello's rhetoric serves to demythify the illusion that the native voice has an autonomous existence outside the purview of elite discourses. At the same time, Tello's (and Candelario's) distinction between archaeological excavation and its Dark Other—sacking or looting—is perhaps a self-reflexive commentary, a parodic mirror image of the author's equivocal relation to the speech of the Other that he scavenges and displays in his novel. Is he the noble archaeologist dedicated to salvage, or the ignoble exploiter? Calendario himself alludes to the duplicity of those who engage his services as a *huaquero* and the process by which what he produces is marked out for foreign consumption:

> If I get an order from the Museum to dig in Montegrande this time I'll screw them up, not like the year before last when I dug up a pile of really fine protonasca pieces and months later when I went to the Museum I didn't see a single one of them because they'd all been sold to foreigners . . .
>
> (Si consigo orden del Museo para excavar en Montegrande esta vez sí los jodo y no como el año antepasado que saqué un montón de piezas finísimas protonasca y a los meses que fui al Museo no vi ni una sola de las que saqué porque toditas las habían negociado para el extranjero . . . ) (37)

The native voice here expresses the self-consciousness of the author who employs the *testimonio* as a venue for making local products exotic and marketable. The supposed authenticity of Candelario's voice is further problematized by allusions to high-culture writers and themes that can only be ascribed to authorial intervention, as for example in this parodic echo of the most famous scene in Proust's *Remembrance of Things Past:* "From all the cat meat I've eaten in my life, I still have the taste in my mouth, I click my tongue against my palate and taste again that richness and just then I remember about Pedro Regalado . . ." (De tanto gato que he comido en mi vida todavía me queda el sabor en la boca, chasqueo la lengua contra el paladar y vuelvo a sentir esa esquisitez, me brota agua limpia, y ahí mismo me acuerdo de Pedro Regalado, 85). With the parodic substitution of cat for Proust's madeleine in Candelario's reminiscence, Martínez defamiliarizes the illusion of the authentic, unmediated native voice. For although Candelario mimics the style of oral narrative, the double-voiced nature of this passage serves to remind the reader that what he is reading is a literary text.

A similar effect is produced when Candelario evokes the classical theme of carpe diem:

> That's the way catastrophe is, it grabs us unawares and—*ñapu*— swallows us whole. That being the case it's natural that I seek pleasure, eating what I've never eaten, doing what I haven't done because it's not fair or reasonable that the world should end forever while a lot of us haven't taken advantage of all that exists for our pleasure and satisfaction.

> (Así es la ruina, el cataclismo, nos agarra desprevenidos y, ñapu, nos engulle sin contemplaciones . . . siendo así es natural que vaya gozando, comiendo lo que no he comido, haciendo lo que no he hecho, porque no es justo ni razonable que se acabe el mundo y muchos no le hayamos sacado el menor provecho en todo lo que hay y existe para el goce y la satisfacción.) (49–50)

Candelario's version of carpe diem suggests that his restless desire that propels him in a constant pursuit of sensual pleasure, his perception of the ruin and decay of his native Coyungo, and his obsession with the art of seduction can be seen in relation to previous texts within a literary tradition. Martínez further disturbs the general tone created by the use of colloquial speech by introducing abrupt and radical changes of style into Candelario's narrative.[47] If throughout Candelario's language is crudely scatological, explicitly sexual, and liberally sprinkled with colloquial expressions and

47. Juan Duchesne discusses the presence of more than one narrative voice in the novel, in "Etnopoética y estrategias discursivas en *Canto de sirena.*"

colorful exclamations such as *ñapu, al tuntún,* and *bundungún,* at times
he waxes unexpectedly lyrical, especially when reflecting on the passage
of time and the stark desolation of Coyungo:

> I look around and see the solitude like an oppressive silence, marked
> by the ashes of the spent fire and the wretched condition of the black
> pots, eaten away, chipped by old age . . . Wherever I look I find the
> rippling of destruction, decay sharpening its teeth, crumbling the dried
> mud covering the reed walls. If I speak, my voice, alive, remains
> trapped in empty silence, spinning around like a lost murmur, whining,
> howling, crying piteously.

> (Miro alrededor y siento la soledad como un silencio opresivo, mar-
> cado por la ceniza del fogón apagado y el aspecto mísero de las
> ollas negras, carcomidas, desboquichadas por la propia vejez . . . Hacia
> donde mire encuentro el escarcio de la destrucción, la roña afilando
> sus dientes, desmenuzando el barro seco que cubre las paredes de
> carrizo. Si hablo mi voz, viva, queda atrapada en el silencio vacío,
> dando vueltas como un murmullo extraviado, quejándose, aullando,
> llorando lastimeramente . . . ) (39)

The inconsistency of the novel's narrative voice points to a fundamental
deceitfulness in Candelario that makes him an unreliable narrator. If the
illusion of truth and the informant's sincerity are conventions of the testimonial genre, Candelario reminds the reader that seduction is an equivocal
art that requires a certain duplicity; as he himself notes: "you can't flirt
without lying . . . what lover isn't a liar? point him out to me so I can see
him for myself" (no hay galanteo sin mentira . . . ¿cuál es ese enamorado
que no es mentiroso?, enséñemelo para conocerlo, para verle su traza, 135).
Candelario's strategy of seduction reflects back on the problematic nature
of the ethnographic interview and the tendency for the native informant to
tell the anthropologist what he wants to hear, to comply with his desire for
the "exotic fruits" of the Other's cultural orchard, the "fruits" that seduce
elite writers like Martínez.

Candelario is, then, by his own account unreliable, not to be trusted. His
relation to authority wavers between compliance and resistance. Although
he seems to have been a reliable servant to his various masters, a loyal
bodyguard to anti-Aprista forces, and an enthusiastic student of Tello's
archaeology, he is just as often involved in subverting authority from
below. His personal vision of the biblical Eden includes a portrait of Adam
as an irreverent rebel against the authority of his Creator: "Adam started

to screw around as soon as he felt the primordial breath on his face and saw the light of the world and got up and on hearing God ask where are you going? answered that he was going to screw around" (Adán empezó a joder apenas sintió el soplo antediluviano en la cara y vio la luz del mundo y se levantó y al escuchar la voz de Dios que le decía ¿a dónde vas? le contestó que iba a joder, 26).

Elsewhere, Candelario reveals his duplicity with respect to authority when he recounts having prepared a meal for workers digging up *huacas,* including Tello, and having thrown in some *chalonas* or dried meat found in the tombs, thus violating a strict code regarding what can and cannot be consumed. Candelario's covert transgressions of authority and his propensity for deceit suggest a resistance to the imposition of authorial control, a refusal to be consumed on the part of the Other that makes the truth claims of *testimonio* problematic.[48] Meanwhile, Martínez appropriates this transgressive voice of his protagonist/informant in order to deploy a transgressive aesthetics of his own with respect to the authorized literary standards of high culture. The crude language and the quasi-pornographic sensibility in some passages of the novel suggest an unexpected relation between the ethnographic imagination and pornography: both share a kind of mesmerizing attention to detail and a voyeuristic focus. With the same kind of minute detail that he devotes to describing the arts of *huaquería* and castration, Candelario records the particulars of his erotic experiences in his diary. The diary is a kind of *mise-en-abime* text within the text, as it reproduces and mirrors the novel's obsessions with the act of seduction.

The regressive circularity of the pornographic imagination returns over and over to the same point only to begin again, repeating its pleasure. Unlike the life history whose structure is generally linear following the chronology of the informant's life, *Siren's Song* has a musical structure, circular and regressive, like a "canto" (song). Themes and anecdotes are prefigured in the text and then taken up again as variations; the story of Candelario's trysts with Marcela Denegri, for example, is alluded to early in the novel, and taken up again in more detail much later. Candelario refers to his birth certificate on page 51 and returns to the involved story of how

48. Lucille Kerr discusses Jesusa's refusal to be consumed by her interlocutor Elena Poniatowska in "Gestures of Authorship: Lying to Tell the Truth in Elena Poniatowska's *Hasta no verte Jesús mío.*"

he went looking for it toward the end of the novel. The text begins with a description of La Plaza in Coyungo and ends with an anecdote that takes place there.

The real voice in *Siren's Song,* then, is clearly not that of a spontaneous, ingenuous native informant but rather that of a writer who, having fantasized the Other's plenitude, is faced with the Other's own incompleteness, his own unquenchable desires. It is the voice of a self-conscious writer who produces and arranges the Other's words to conform to his literary design; as Candelario puts it: "in a tomb, every stone, every piece of stoneware has its reason to be there, you can't just put things any old way" (en una huaca, cada piedra, cada arenisca, tiene su motivo, no se puede trabajar a la diabla, 109). Martínez's novel is in a sense a *testimonio* about the writing of a *testimonio,* and as such constitutes a transgressive rewriting of the genre.

The longevity of the *testimonio* in the Latin American canon contributes to its vulnerability to the parodist, as with any genre. But despite the increasing suspicion with which the apparently unadulterated native voice as presented by an anthropologist/scribe has been received by critics, Latin American writers continue to produce, and to be seduced by, these texts. While in North America the long and continuing tradition of native American testimonial autobiography has been superseded by the contemporary creative flowering of ethnic autobiography, the product of a multicultural postmodern sensibility, "lives" in Latin America are still being produced by a third party, and the indigenous voice has developed little or no autonomy.[49]

In 1980, the Mexican anthropologist and novelist Carlo Antonio Castro published *Siluetas mexicanas,* a text that includes two *testimonios:* "Che Ndu, Ejidatario Chinanteco," and "Lupe, La de Altotonga." The reader of this work could imagine that thirty years had not passed since the publication of Ricardo Pozas's *Juan Pérez Jolote.* Nevertheless, in an epigraph Castro quotes from a personal letter written to him by Ernesto Cardenal, in which the Nicaraguan poet marvels at the text's lyricism:

> I read with great interest—and more than interest, with great admiration—Lupe's beautiful story . . . I was amazed at the poetic beauty of the language, poetry like that of Homer or the *Popol Vuh,* much

---

49. On ethnic autobiography in the U.S., see Michael M. J. Fischer, "Ethnicity and the Postmodern Arts of Memory."

superior to a large part of our contemporary high culture, that has tried to be of the people like this and has failed. And here is an Indian girl who with unconscious ease succeeds much better than we do . . . [50]

In Latin America the transition from *testimonio* to autobiography has not been accomplished, due to the continued prevalence of illiteracy among the masses and the persistence of inequality and oppression that the *testimonio* eloquently sublimates as aesthetic expression. Yet the myth of the native voice as natural poetry endures, and is evoked, remarkably, even by committed Marxists like Cardenal—and Barnet.[51]

50. Carlo Antonio Castro, *Siluetas mexicanas,* 63.
51. For a Marxist critique of Latin American writers' folkloristic vision of popular culture, see Silverio Muñoz, *José María Arguedas y el mito de la salvación por la cultura.*

# 5

## THE "I" OF THE ANTHROPOLOGIST
### Allegories of Fieldwork in Darcy Ribeiro's *Maíra*

Darcy Ribeiro, the Brazilian anthropologist, educator, politician, and out-spoken social critic, was born in 1922, studied anthropology as a young man, and in 1946 began a period of fieldwork among the Amazon Indi-ans of Central Brazil that continued for approximately ten years. Ribeiro founded and for a time directed the *Museo do Indio* in Rio de Janeiro, and became a professor of ethnology. In 1954 he turned to education, founding the University of Brasília, and rose to the position of minister of education. In 1964, Ribeiro was forced into exile following the overthrow of João Goulart, which brought a military dictatorship to power. He spent the years from 1964 to 1975 creating and advising universities in various countries in Central and South America.[1]

Ribeiro was trained as an anthropologist in the functionalist tradition of British social anthropology. In this tradition, individual cultures were studied as discrete, organic structures in the manner of the natural sciences, treating each culture as a timeless, isolatable unit. In social anthropology, as in American cultural anthropology, fieldwork became the primary task for the professional anthropologist. The model was Malinowski, who, reacting against the "armchair" methods of scholars like Sir James Frazer, insisted that the fieldwork anthropologist's goal was to immerse himself in the life of a particular native group for an extended period of time and then

---

1. See Ribeiro's three-page autobiographical sketch in *Sobre o obvio,* 9–12.

document the results of painstaking research and close observation in the form of a monograph. Ribeiro's extensive writings in anthropology include the requisite monograph, on the Kadiwéu. He has also written social satire, several books on education, and a multivolume work on Latin American and Brazilian civilization. In 1975, Ribeiro returned to Brazil, was elected vice governor of Rio de Janeiro in 1982, and once again turned his attention to problems of education. His first novel, *Maíra,* appeared in 1976, and has been widely translated.[2]

In retrospect, Ribeiro laments the sterility of the depoliticized, dehistoricized functionalism he embraced at the outset of his career, and its indifference to the fate of individual Indian groups threatened by Brazilian expansion into their territory: "Brainwashed, indoctrinated without being aware of it, we were immersed in tasks that led to a cold scientism as an end in itself, apart from any social problematic." He also criticizes the objectification of the Indian in functionalist studies, the look from outside, the scientific gaze: "they were always the external object that we observed from the outside like a thing."[3] Ribeiro's novel *Maíra* is a modernist, fragmented text that repudiates the documentary realism of the functionalist monograph. While the monograph intends to be an authoritative appropriation of cultures as holistic, internally consistent, and transparently interpretable, the fragmentation and the refusal of totalization in *Maíra* reflects the anthropologist's perception of an Other who is ultimately elusive, closed to the penetrating gaze of the scientist.

Ribeiro began his extended contact with the Indian tribes of the Amazon region as an anthropologist employed by the *Serviço de Proteção aos Indios* to study the effects of their policy of "pacification" and the degree of assimilation achieved as a result of such policies. His experience turned Ribeiro into an opponent of Indian assimilation to the national culture, convincing him that the integrity of the individual tribes should be preserved.[4] Rather than becoming assimilated, he found, the Indians were becoming more and more marginalized and their traditional ways of life were disintegrating.

Ribeiro confesses that the years he spent among the Amazon Indians (1946–1955) were "the best ten years of his life."[5] This subjective

---

2. Following *Maíra,* Ribeiro published three other novels: *O mulo* (1981), *Utopia selvagem* (1982), and *Migo: romance* (1988).

3. Ribeiro, *Testemunho,* 35, 42.

4. See his account in the prologue to *Fronteras indígenas de la civilización,* 3–16.

5. Ribeiro, *Sobre o obvio,* 9.

experience of the Other is necessarily excluded from his anthropological texts, but haunts the margins as that which the discourse of social science represses. In an analysis of the rhetoric of ethnographic discourse, Michel de Certeau discusses the strategies of power and exclusion involved in the West's objectifying of the Other in writing. Such discourse about the Other, according to Certeau, constitutes its authority by entrapping the "primitive" in its scriptural economy, and in the process necessarily excludes, banishes, what resists its grasp: the primitive voice, uncanny in its resistance to capture; the primitive economy of excess, inimical to the Western economy of production, work, and profit; and the erotic attraction of the primitive body for the Western observer.[6]

Ribeiro's writing about the Other in his novel *Maíra* is a way of writing about the Self and its conflictive relation to the "primitive," subverting the scriptural conquests undertaken by Ribeiro the anthropologist. The repressed experiences of the intimate Self—doubts, fantasies, guilt feelings— that have been exiled to the margins of scientific discourse as it seeks to objectify the Other, return in the novel where the authoritative "I" of the anthropologist gives way to shifting and numerous voices.

At times the narrator is "we," the collective voice of the Mairun tribe. At other times, a distanced third-person narrator, similar to that which Angel Rama identifies in Arguedas's *Deep Rivers* as an anthropological voice, is employed.[7] In an autobiographical chapter, "Egosum," the first-person narrator is identifiably Ribeiro himself. Other voices in the novel include those of the twin gods of creation in the Mairun cosmology, a third-person mythic voice that narrates Mairun creation myths, and the first-person voices of the novel's main characters. In several chapters, the twin gods Maíra and Micura enter into the minds of characters in order to provoke them to narrate their thoughts. The use of shifting and numerous voices in *Maíra* reflects Ribeiro's sense of the multiplicity of cultural and individual perspectives and the unstable position of the anthropologist for whom "the jungle is cacophonous, filled with too many voices."[8]

In *Maíra,* the plight of the Amazon Indians is reflected in a fictional tribe, an archetype that the novelist creates using a pastiche of intertribal

6. See de Certeau's "Ethno-Graphy: Speech, or the Space of the Other: Jean de Léry," in *The Writing of History,* 209–43.
7. Angel Rama, *Transculturación narrativa,* 270–79.
8. Clifford, *Predicament of Culture,* 102–3.

cultural variations.[9] Since Ribeiro's profession made him keenly aware of differences among the various Indian groups, his use of a generic Amazonian tribe in the novel suggests an allegorical intention. In fact, as I will show, the characters and situations in *Maíra* represent allegories of the fieldwork experience and of the encounter between Self and Other that underlies the anthropological project.

*Maíra* unfolds as a mystery to be solved: a white woman, Alma, has been found dead on a beach in a remote area that is home to the Mairun. The authorities seek to solve the (possible) crime, but the novel ends without a satisfactory explanation for the woman's fate. Through his plotting of an unsolved murder mystery, Ribeiro raises questions about the impossibility of knowing the Other, and about the position of the anthropologist as akin to that of a police investigator aggressively seeking information and clear-cut rational answers. The chapters that plot the police investigation alternate with mythic narratives of Mairun creation myths and with the central story the novel develops involving the protagonists Avá/Isaías and Alma.

Avá is torn between his identity as a Mairun Indian by birth and his experiences as a student of theology in Brazil and Europe. Sent away from his native tribe by priests as a child, Avá takes on another identity—Isaías—but feels the weight of tradition pulling him back to his origins. The novel plots his return to a people whose lifestyle he can no longer fully share, and who treat him as the outsider he cannot help but be.

The character Avá is based on a real-life figure whose ambiguous status as neither insider nor outsider Ribeiro found poignant and exemplary of the clash between the white world and the Indian tribes that stripped the Indians of their cultural autonomy, but failed to provide them with alternatives. The Kadiwéu, for example, are for Ribeiro "a people caught between two worlds and marginalized by both: the world of the old ways, become unfeasible, and the world of the nation that surrounds them where they have no place except through self-negation."[10]

In "Egosum," a chapter in *Maíra*, Ribeiro states that the model for Avá was a Borôro named Tiago whom he watched perform a traditional ceremony: he was feathering the bones of his daughter, who died of smallpox. What strikes Ribeiro is that the man consoled himself by reciting

9. For specific references, see Susane Klengel's excellent article *"Maíra de Darcy Ribeiro: la búsqueda de lo auténtico."*

10. Darcy Ribeiro, *Kadiwéu: Ensaios etnológicos sobre o saber, o azar e a beleza,* 8.

a prayer in Latin.[11] Ribeiro tells this man's story in his *Fronteras indígenas de la civilización* (Indigenous borders of civilization) as well. Describing a funeral ceremony for the last great Borôro chieftain, Cadete, who died during a flu epidemic in 1953 that decimated the tribe, he notes that the man had studied for some years in Cuiabá, sent by priests who hoped to cultivate a future missionary. At the funeral, though he appeared to be exactly like the other members of his tribe, Ribeiro observes that he deviated from tradition by concentrating on his personal grief over the death of his daughter rather than on the collective grief of the tribe.[12]

That the Borôro fails to mourn Cadete, mourning instead his daughter, reflects for Ribeiro the disintegration of the tribal way of life and its communal rituals that can no longer offer solace in the face of the dominant national culture's penetration. Like the Borôro, the Mairun in *Maíra* are suffering the effects of what he calls detribalization. A funeral ceremony for the chieftain Anacã that becomes a leitmotif in the novel retains the flavor of tradition, but present circumstances prevent the full realization of all aspects of the ritual:

> Already we should have danced the Coraci-Iaci, but we cannot. It is the solemn dance of the Jaguar, the dance of the chieftains. Without a chieftain, how could we have danced it? (29)

> (Já devíamos ter dançado o Coraci-Iaci, mas não podemos. Essa é a dança solene do Jaguar, a dança dos tuxavas. Sem tuxava como havíamos de dança-la?) (47)

Like this lament that *takes the place of* the prescribed ritual of mourning, writing in the novel becomes for Ribeiro a ritual of mourning both for the lost integrity of the Mairun tribe before contact with the white man, and for the lost plenitude of experience before recourse to the supplement of writing. The attempt to recover through writing what is irrecoverable infuses the novel with an elegiac nostalgia. Johannes Fabian notes that all ethnography is autobiographical in the sense that it records the anthropologist's experience of the Other as part of his own past.[13] Ribeiro's portrayal of the Mairun tribe as living a present immeasurably

---

11. Darcy Ribeiro, *Maíra*, 209; in the translation, 176. Subsequent page references to the novel will be to the English translation first and then to the original Portuguese.

12. Ribeiro, *Maíra*, 209; *Fronteras indígenas*, 287.

13. Johannes Fabian, *Time and the Other: How Anthropology Makes Its Object*. See in particular 71–104.

diminished with respect to its paradisiacal past cannot be divorced from his personal sense of loss—"the best ten years"—and of his own mortality. The past is what is valuable, and lost forever, for both the Mairun and the anthropologist. Significantly, the novel begins with the discovery of a corpse in a chapter entitled "A morte" (Death). In the second chapter the last great Mairun chieftain, Anacã, bids farewell to his people as he senses his approaching death. Following his death and burial, ritual mourning for Anacã, a metaphor for the writing itself, continues as a leitmotif through many chapters.

Like the Borôro Indian Tiago who mourns his daughter, the protagonist Avá in *Maíra* is raised by missionaries to be a priest, sent to Europe, and finally attempts unsuccessfully and tragically to resume the life he had abandoned. Ribeiro's most expressive writing about the Other in texts otherwise characterized by the discourse of scientific objectivity (graphs, tables, etc.), like *Indigenous Borders of Civilization,* is devoted to this kind of tragic figure. The Indian girl Korikrã, for example, adopted by the German doctor Hugo Gensh, internalized the whites' rejection of Indian ways so completely that when as a grown woman she is brought to meet her people, finally "pacified," her reaction is one of fear and revulsion.[14]

Like Tiago and Korikrã, Avá returns to his Mairun village a divided being who, through contact with the world outside, has lost the sensibility that would allow him to live the Mairun lifestyle without questioning it. The perspective of his experiences on the outside makes it impossible for him to accept the persistence of Mairun ways of life that seem to contribute to their decline and reinforce their marginal status. In other words, he sees and judges their behavior as an outsider would, criticizing the excess of energy they waste, in his view, making baskets, nets, and pots when they could be attending to more serious matters, and the informal, joking way in which they treat sacred lore (277–78; 318–19).

The Mairun worldview is in conflict with that of the world bearing down on them that Avá parrots unawares in his annoyed observation of what the Mairun lack: a sense of the utility or the uselessness of certain practices, and a sense of piety regarding their myths. Juca, the half-breed son of a white

14. Anthropologists have traditionally been fascinated by those who cross the border between Self and Other: anthropologists who "go native," captives, or natives who find themselves inexorably drawn into the white man's world. On the marginalized native, see for example Theodora Kroeber's *Ishi in Two Worlds: A Biography of the Last Wild Indian in North America.*

man and an Indian woman, scorns the Indians for their indifference to the commercial values that would make them players like himself rather than victims of an exploitation economy. They have no money, he complains, because "these idiots have the custom of burying with the dead everything that belongs to him" (117; 146). Juca's system for recruiting Mairun labor—showering them with "gifts" for which they then become indebted—was originally used coercively by the Putumayo rubber gatherers and eventually by the *Serviço de Proteção aos Indios* during its "pacification" campaign. Juca's entrepreneurism represents the breakdown of the communal spirit and its replacement by a spirit of individualism and mutual exploitation. He is the benevolent pacifier's dark Other.

The Mairun in Ribeiro's novel are in mourning for their last great chieftain Anacã, who cannot be replaced because there has ceased to be a legitimate line of succession. Avá is by birth next in line, but his extended existence outside the tribe has rendered him incapable of the leadership qualities necessary to be a Mairun chief. Following a chapter recounting the mythic deeds of the Mairun god Maíra, Avá's inability even to catch a fish is an ironic counterpoint. Like Tiago's wife, Avá's Mairun wife, Inimá, ignores him, sleeping with all except her husband. Avá's own father, Remui, the guide of souls, laments his son's worthlessness as a potential leader. Avá's plan to introduce the Mairun into an economy of production and profit betrays his fall away from a paradisiacal economy of spending and excess indifferent to the production and profit that motivate Western economies.

Avá makes the journey back from "civilization" to his people in the company of Alma, a white woman who feels compelled to redeem her troubled life by becoming a missionary. Once in contact with the Mairun tribe, however, she loses herself and her sense of mission to the sensual and immediate pulse of the Mairun rhythm of life. Alma is examined and undressed by the curious Mairun, who have never seen a white woman, in a kind of anthropology-in-reverse, with the natives doing the examining, looking, and probing. This seductive "lesson in intimate anthropology" (225; 261) identifies the native position as object of the West's colonizing gaze with that of the feminine as passive object of the male gaze.[15]

15. Mary Louise Pratt identifies what I have called "anthropology in reverse" as a "sentimental commonplace" or trope in travel writing "whereby the natives try to undress the foreigners to determine their humanity and, symbolically, level the difference between them." In "Fieldwork in Common Places," 37.

Alma represents a recurring fantasy of anthropologists in the field: to be totally accepted, embraced by a native society to the point of becoming one of them. Avá envies Alma's uninhibited immersion in the everyday life of the Mairun, but danger lurks in the dissolution of stable cultural and ego boundaries, and Alma dies before, or in the process of, giving birth to twins fathered by a Mairun.

Alma becomes a "mirixorã," or a woman who, since she belongs sexually to no one, belongs to everyone. Having lost her way in the city and turned to drugs, casual sex, and psychotherapy, Alma finds herself and is reborn as "a priestess of love" among the Mairun. Her sensual rebirth, like Kate's in D. H. Lawrence's *The Plumed Serpent,* connotes the submission of the rational "I," the ego, to what that position has repressed. As a woman, Alma can play out the anthropologist's desire for the eroticized body of the primitive while avoiding the connotation of male penetration violating the Other's body, reenacting the original rape of Conquest. Because she gives herself, submits, is taken, Alma represents the anthropologist's conflictive desire to renounce the (phallic) thrust of scientific discourse, to be seduced by the primitive.

Avá desires Alma, but his impotence, his incapacity for intimacy, condemns him to gaze at her from a distance: he "remains hidden in the tall grass nearby . . . he takes an obscure delight in furtive, stolen, shameful glances . . . It is not lust, perhaps, but perhaps it is" (fica escondido na macega . . . Tira algum gozo recôndito desta mirada furtiva, roubada, envergonhada . . . Não é desejo, talvez, mas talvez seja, 159; 191). This voyeuristic looking as a guilty activity that may or may not be desire is clearly suggestive of the fieldwork situation, where the conflict between a desire for intimacy and the necessity to maintain the distance between Self and Other underlie the anthropological encounter. Ribeiro suggests that the intimacy he managed to achieve among the Kadiwéu prevented him from being a good anthropologist:

> With them I learned that only a profound emotional identification can break down the barriers to communication, allowing a stranger to penetrate the intimacy of a people's vision of the world. In reality, my studies of the Kadiwéu aren't better than they are only because my qualifications as an anthropologist were very precarious. I attained, with many of them, such a high level of communication and intimacy that I achieved about the most that an anthropologist can aspire to in his effort to see the world through the eyes of those he is studying.[16]

16. Ribeiro, *Kadiwéu,* 12.

Again, true intimacy with and knowledge of the Other is seen as incompatible with the strict objectivity required of the social scientist. Ribeiro's idyllic view of his fieldwork experience is belied, however, in the confessional chapter "Egosum":

> Those months of inescapable living together in the communal hut almost drove me mad. Only within the four walls of a prison cell have I felt so confined and constrained. Conditioned to live in houses with walls and doors to isolate ourselves, to hide ourselves, we can't stand that ceaseless communion among Indians, day and night, constantly living a communal life . . . Oh, those times so long ago when I tried to behave like I were them, learning to live the life of others but feeling hopelessly withdrawn into and clinging to myself. (177–78)
>
> (Aqueles meses de convívio enelutável da maloca, quase me enlouqueceram. Só na prisão das quatro paredes me senti assim contido e constrangido. Condicionados a viver em casas com muros e portas para nos isolar, para nos esconder, não suportamos aquela comunicação índia sem fim, de dia e de noite, vivendo sempre uma vida totalmente comungante . . . O! tempos meus longínquos aqueles em que eu me exercia como gente, aprendendo a viver a existência dos outros, mas sentindo-me irremediavelmente atado e atolado no fundo de mim.) (211–12)

Here the "I" intrudes on the scene, dispelling the illusion of a collective intimacy, underscoring the irremediable distance between Self and Other. That Alma's transgressive crossing of the border causes her to lose her life suggests that for Ribeiro the crossing is a dangerous one marked by desire and the threat of annihilation. In "Egosum" he recalls a situation in which an obsessive desire to bridge that distance leads him to risk his life. According to Urubu custom, a person who has suffered great emotional pain, as at the death of a loved one, may declare himself *inharon*. When this occurs, all others flee the village and he remains alone to take out his grief in a violent rage. Ribeiro is overcome by the desire to see this man's face, and he makes his way back to the village obsessed by the idea. The *inharon* fascinates Ribeiro because he represents losing oneself in an absolute passion of rage by divesting oneself of the limits of rationality that inhibit desire. Their confrontation is an uncanny experience for Ribeiro, who recognizes in the pure excess of the *inharon* a shadow figure of what he has repressed. As Michel de Certeau suggests, "scientific 'reason' is indissolubly wedded to the reality that it meets again as its shadow and its other, at the very moment when it is excluding it."[17] This anecdote that reveals what the distanced, rational voice of the anthropologist represses is also an allegory about the nature of anthropology, as the violence of the *inharon* comes face to face with another kind of violence: the transgressive presence of the anthropologist intruding on his most intimate private moments. Yet beyond this there does occur a fleeting moment of mutual recognition between the *inharon* and the anthropologist, whose culturally determined ways of confronting death—the ritual excess of the *inharon* versus the West's channeling of anguish into the productive economy of writing—reveal their shared impotence and rage at the outrage that is mortality. The encounter is thus a kind of parable about how the anthropologist meets up with the confirmation of his own fears and desires in the Other.[18]

The anthropologist is drawn to the Other's sensual world of intimacy wherein the rational, controlling "I" ceases to repress desire. The voice of the Mairun becomes a counterdiscourse in the novel, setting the sensuality of the Indian communal festivals against the repressively antisensual rituals of Christianity:

> On through the night, the day and the next night, we eat, converse and laugh; we eat, we drink, we walk about, we shit; we eat, we drink, we belch, we spit, we vomit, we converse and laugh; we eat, we make love, we dance, we fuck, we sleep . . . (78)

> (Através da noite, do dia, e da noite que vem, comemos, falamos e rimos; comemos, bebemos, andamos, cagamos; comemos, bebemos, arrotamos, cuspimos, vomitamos, falamos e rimos, comemos, namoramos, dançamos, fodemos, dormimos . . . ) (103)

The Mairun voice is plural and focused on the body, its functions, and its various pleasures: the taste of food, the joy of sex, the communal delight in laughter and song. The twin gods participate in the Mairun festivities, eating, laughing, and making love to Mairun girls. There is no place in the scene for that which remains aloof, the "I" that holds back, that doesn't give itself entirely. The Mairun festival fascinates the anthropologist as a

17. Michel de Certeau, *The Writing of History,* 40.

18. The ritual excess of the *inharon* recalls the potlatch ceremonies that fascinated Georges Bataille as, in Michele Richman's words, "the means by which the established order is periodically disrupted, and the anguishing confrontation with death symbolized in the destruction of goods ritually dramatized." See Bataille's *La Part maudite* and Richman's commentary in *Reading Georges Bataille: Beyond the Gift,* 16–23.

spectacle of sheer excess that cannot be "brought back" through writing, "ephemeral and irrecoupable, unexploitable moments that will neither be regained nor redeemed." Festival and ritual remain outside the productive economy of the West and of writing, "a senseless speech ravishing Western discourse, but one which, because of that very fact, generates a productive science of meaning and objects that endlessly writes." The anthropologist's project of textualization clashes with that of the Indians who "spend their time celebrating, in pure expression that neither preserves nor accrues profit, in a present eternal time *off*, a pure excess."[19]

In contrast, Christians lead "[d]ry ashes of lives, without honey or salt. Hard lives, with blind affections, and clipped desires" ([s]ecas vidas de cinzas, sem doce nem sal. Vidas duras, de carinhos segadas, de desejos podadas, 135; 165). The Christian God is a distant one who unlike Maíra and Micura keeps above the fray watching panoptically "do alto." He is to be invoked solemnly, as in Avá's prayer juxtaposed ironically to the Mairun festivities: "O God of Rome who illuminates me not / O God of Heaven who seest me not / My God, whom I invoke in vain" (O' Deus de Roma que não me iluminou / O' Deus do Céu que não me viu / Meu Deus, que invoquei em vão, 79; 105).

Religious symbolism pervades *Maíra,* which is divided into four sections labeled "Antiphony," "Homily," "Gospel," and "Corpus." The spirit of apocalypse runs through the novel and is explicitly invoked in the sermons of the black preacher Xisto who finally, taking apocalyptic imagery to its literal extreme, goes mad. Other authority figures associated with Christianity are equally corrupt or morally blind: the North American evangelist Bob and his Bible-translating wife Gertrude; the Fathers at the Mission. The novel juxtaposes the sense of playfulness in Mairun myth to the high seriousness of Christian liturgy.

Avá's Christian name "Isaías" is ironic, for the prodigal Mairun is a failed prophet (like Xisto) who returns without revelations, and without the faith in a just God and His absolute Truth that empowered his biblical namesake. Ribeiro, like Avá, yearns for revelations of a Truth that are not forthcoming, because faith is lacking:

> There they shine, I've seen them: baroque, vociferous prophets. One among them speaks to me without pause or end. It is he with mouth burned by the word of God: Isaías.

19. Certeau, *The Writing of History,* 227, 236, 228.

Oh fierce fires that burn me not! I had wished for the total blaze of absolute truth, I who knew only smoking embers and the bitterness of gall diluted by the sea. (179–80)

(Ali luzem, eu vi, barrocos profetas vociferantes. Entre eles um me fala sem pausa nem termo. E o da boca queimada pela palavra de Deus: Isaías.
    O feros fogos que não me queimam. Quisera o fogo inteiro da verdade toda, eu que só conheci brasas fumegantes e o gosto de fel diluído no mar.) (213)[20]

Like Isaías and Alma, the police investigator Nonato dos Anjos is an alter ego of the author, and part of his allegorical self-questioning. James Clifford compares the anthropologist to a police investigator and anthropology to interrogation in his study on Marcel Griaule: "Griaule's tactics are varied, but they have in common an active, aggressive posture not unlike the judicial process of interrogation." Griaule himself makes this analogy explicit: "The role of the person sniffing out social facts is often comparable to that of a detective or examining magistrate. The fact is the crime, the interlocutor the guilty party; all the society's members are accomplices."[21]

Griaule's "tactics" during his fieldwork among the Dogon were based on a conception of the Other as the passive object of the anthropologist's aggressive will to power and knowledge. He sought to impose his own unquestioned positional superiority and oblige the native to relinquish cultural truths as if they were artifacts—and artifacts, as "booty," were expected to be handed over as well. Griaule sought to expose contradictions among informants through aggressive questioning in order to banish undecidability or ambiguity, and to arrive at an ultimate "Truth" about the Dogon.

In contrast to Griaule, Ribeiro portrays the Other in his novel as an impenetrable enigma. Avá questions the possibility that an outsider can decipher his people's mysteries: "Whoever looks on this from outside, how will he understand? Only we, those from within, can know. Even so, only

---

20. Isaiah's prophecy that a child Immanuel (God is with us) would be born to "almah" (Hebrew for young woman) as a sign confirming Judah's temporary liberation from its aggressors, echoes ironically in the death of Alma's twins. The deaths also negate the optimism of the mestizo birth in José de Alencar's *Iracema*; see Roberto Ventura, "Literature, Anthropology, and Popular Culture in Brazil: From José de Alencar to Darcy Ribeiro."

21. Clifford, *Predicament of Culture*, 73. My comments on Griaule are based on Clifford's discussion.

more or less. The Mairuns are a deep and secretive people" (Quem olhar de fora, como há de entender? Só nós, os de dentro, nos sabemos. Assim mesmo, mais ou menos. Mairun é gente disfarçada, 40; 60).

Nonato's modus operandi is typically bureaucratic in that his vision focuses on surface data and utterly fails to perceive what lies beyond his limited visual field. He records the testimony of the Swiss naturalist who found the body, and exhumes the dead woman's bones (in violation of Mairun custom) but finds no evidence of violence. He examines the Indians with a clinical eye and produces a report that mimics the naturalistic strain of anthropological discourse:

> The general appearance of these Indians is good; they have good teeth . . . and good skin, free of traces of illness except for pockmarks. Many of the bigger youths here would make excellent recruits. They are tall and broad-shouldered . . . their faces are open and pleasant . . . It is a pity that nearly all the Indians are potbellied . . . the result of their staple diet of manioc flour . . . (195)

> (O aspecto geral dos índios e bom, bons dentes . . . Boa pele, limpa de sinais de doenças, exceto bexigas em alguns. Uns quantos rapagões daqui dariam excelente recrutas. São altos e espadaúdos . . . e exibem umas caras abertas, sorridentes, francas, que dão gosto . . . O lamentável é que quase todos esses índios têm barrigas estufadas. . . . é a dieta de mandioca . . . ) (228)

The investigator's eye is distant yet intimate in its focus; his photographic gaze searches the intimate spaces of the Mairun anatomy while maintaining a controlling distance.[22] Nonato interrogates the Mairun but is unable to interpret their responses as they don't conform to the knowledge-producing paradigm—the interrogation—that he attempts to enact:

> I sought to further my investigations by questioning the Indians about the death, the pregnancy, the birth, the reasons for her going to the beach alone to die. They either changed the subject or would not reply. (197)

> (Procurei levar adiante ali mesmo minha indagação junto aos índios, fazendo-lhes perguntas sobre a morta, sobre a gravidez, sobre o ato do parto, sobre a razão por que foi parir sozinha na praia. Eles desconversavam ou não diziam nada.) (231–32)

---

22. Michael Taussig calls this "the colonizing eye" in *Shamanism, Colonialism, and the Wild Man: A Study in Terror and Healing,* 113.

Nonato's investigation is based on his need to discover an ultimate and unitary truth to report to his superiors—a truth that he does not find, because it does not exist as such. As Avá suggests: "The truth is not to be found in only one place. And it is not a single thing. It is everywhere; it is multiple, dispersed, and contradictory" (A verdade não está num só lugar . . . é múltipla, dispersa e contraditória, 320; 370). Nonato's conclusion that the mysterious death was a tragic accident is verisimilar in strictly factual terms but is nevertheless a misreading of the situation because it fails to perceive the web of ambiguity that the novel weaves around Alma's death. Perhaps Alma dies because help with birthing is based on kinship ties and, despite her intimacy with the Mairun, she is ultimately an outsider condemned by custom to give birth alone.

There is also the suggestion in the novel that Alma, who cares for the Mairun by bringing them medicine from the Mission, is considered an *oxim,* or sorcerer. It is customary among the Mairun to attack and kill an *oxim* at the height of his glory or if he fails to cure. When the Mairun child Cori is bitten by a snake, she is brought before the *oxim* Teidju but he cannot save her. In a fury the people violently attack and dismember the *oxim.* Avá thinks to himself that Alma may be considered an *oxim,* but perhaps out of envy or sexual jealousy, he fails to warn Alma about her possibly violent fate. Although Nonato considers Avá to be a murder suspect, he of course remains unaware that Avá may be considered morally culpable in the sense that his knowledge of Mairun custom might have saved her. Another hidden clue that Nonato misreads is Elias's comment that the Mairun call Alma "Mosaingar." Elias, a bureaucrat in charge of the FUNAI (National Indian Foundation) post, recognizes Mosaingar to be a religious name but is unaware of the implications of the Mairun calling Alma by this name. In a previous chapter relating Mairun myths of creation, Mosaingar is identified as the bearer of the twin gods Maíra and Micura. Perhaps the Mairun considered Alma's pregnancy to be supernatural, part of a divine plan. Alma herself fails to understand what her lover Jaguar attempts to communicate to her about her condition. Finally, when Alma's body is found, it has been painted red and black, the same colors used in painting the dead chieftain Anacã. None of these mysteriously suggestive clues, however, add up to a coherent picture that would resolve the enigma. In Nonato's failed investigation of the "crime"—which may or may not have been committed—Ribeiro implicitly criticizes a stance toward the Other, a mode of inquiry that inevitably fails to see the essential despite its energetic accumulation of data, clues, and interviews with various "informants."

In *Maíra,* the "I" of the anthropologist is shown to be now a bureaucrat, now a voyeur, now a lost soul in search of redemption, now a mortal in search of eternal truths. For Ribeiro, the inevitable extinction of the Amazon Indian tribes prefigures in a way his own death. He carries the image of the Mairun world inside him like a talisman, as does Avá:

> For me, my Mairun village, during the many years of my exile, existed only within me, in my memory. It was a void in time, way back in the past, that I would revive daily, recollecting it in every detail so that it would never die within me. (46)

> (Para mim, minha aldeia mairum nos anos tantos desse meu desterro, só existiu dentro de mim, na lembrança. Era um oco no tempo, lá atrás, no passado, que eu reavivia diariamente, recordando em cada detalhe para que não apagasse, nem morresse em mim.) (66)

When the Mairun god Maíra laments, "Without them, who would remember, who would praise me?" (Sem eles quem me-há-de-lembrar, louvar? 309; 355) he expresses the anthropologist's nightmare: that what he has devoted his life to preserving—the core of his being—is destined to oblivion. Underlying the novel's requiem for a dying tribe is the anthropologist's anxious awareness of his own mortality: "Oh life that trickles away absentmindedly, like sand between the fingers of time, sifting through my hand even the memory of the feel of my past. We endure only, if at all, through the usury of the memory of others until the evening of ultimate oblivion" (Ai vida que esvai distraída, entre os dedos da hora, tirando da mão até a memória do tato dos meus idos. Só persistimos, se tanto, na usura da memória alheia, á véspera do longo esquecimento, 180; 213).

In an introduction to *Kadiwéu,* Ribeiro recounts a story about how he was given the tribal name Bet'rra-yegi by the Kadiwéu. One day as he was lying in a hammock reading a book about the tribe written in the nineteenth century by the ethnologist Guido Boggiani, his Kadiwéu companions become curious and start to examine the book, amazed by the photographs recognizably of themselves together with someone they identify as Bet'rra:

> Immediately one of the old women shouted: *It's Ligui.* She took the book from me, sat down on the ground surrounded by the others,

speaking and gesturing with growing emotion. Then a man approached me to ask who had given me those papers with so many things that belonged to them and with the venerable Ligui's picture. I tried to explain that it was a book. Then I spoke of the author: an Italian ethnologist who half a century before had lived for a time among the Kadiwéu. The man translated my words and spoke with the women until one of them, Anoã, exclaimed: *Why it's Bet'rra.* From then on, in a confused dialogue in Portuguese and *guaikuru,* the situation was becoming clarified and complicated. The final understanding was that I was a kind of grandnephew of Boggiani who had returned, decades later, to visit the Kadiwéu.[23]

Ribeiro goes on to explain to them that Boggiani (Bet'rra), who had "gone native" to the point of taking a Kadiwéu wife, was killed by an enemy tribe while walking in the jungle. The Kadiwéu women then invent a song that they will sing about Bet'rra whenever they find themselves in the presence of the book. In this recognition scene, the anthropologist and the Kadiwéu create a space where collective memory and the book converge, as the recognition of Bet'rra speaks for a kind of continuity that extends collective memory through generations. In the anthropologist's own culture, this kind of personal immortality is only possible through the books he writes. Ribeiro, dubbed Bet'rra-yegi (grandnephew of Bet'rra) by the Kadiwéu, fantasizes that like Bet'rra he too will live on eternally in their memory—but only, of course, if they survive.

23. Ribeiro, *Kadiwéu,* 11.

# 6

## SA(L)VAGE ETHNOGRAPHY
### The Cannibalistic Imagination in Juan José Saer's *El entenado*

In *Culture and Truth,* Renato Rosaldo discusses a syndrome he calls "imperialist nostalgia," a kind of nostalgia that affects those representatives of Western culture—government officials, anthropologists in the field—who witness the changes caused by the imperialist project of colonizing the Other's territory, and then mourn the passing of the very cultural groups and practices that their own presence helps doom to extinction. Those afflicted with "imperialist nostalgia" fantasize that the past life of the native group whose transformation they abhor was a time of pristine, uncorrupted authenticity spoiled by the intrusion of historical time.[1] Addressing more or less the same phenomenon, Claude Lévi-Strauss denounces as a kind of duplicitous fraud the tendency of those nostalgic for forms of life disappearing from the modern industrialized world to collect and sanctify relics from the premodern Other's past (and present) in museums, in collections of folklore, in ethnographies. Western society attempts to repair the irreparable damage it has done to non-Western peoples by "pretend[ing] to itself that it is investing them with nobility at the very time when it is completing their destruction." For Lévi-Strauss, the Western world's destroy-and-then-salvage mentality reflects "the need feverishly to appease the nostalgiac cannibalism of history with the shadows of those that history has already destroyed."[2]

1. Rosaldo, *Culture and Truth,* 68–87.
2. Lévi-Strauss, *Tristes Tropiques,* 31.

Lévi-Strauss suggests that this nostalgic appropriation is a form of cannibalism, an aggressive, imperialist ingesting of the Other to feed the Self's desires. In *El entenado* (*The Witness*), Juan José Saer situates the phenomenon discussed in historical terms by Rosaldo and Lévi-Strauss in the realm of metaphysics, where the imperialist West becomes the imperialist Self. The novel invokes the historical moment of the Conquest in order to inscribe the Europeans' violent appropriation of the indigenous Other, the natives' ritual cannibalistic ingestion of Others, and the narrator's ethnographic writing about the *colastiné* tribe, in the context of contemporary discourses on subjectivity, Otherness, and language.

In the philosophical tradition that descends from Hegel through Sartre and Lacan, the Self/Other relation has been articulated in terms of the Self's desire for an Other that eludes his grasp, an Other whose irremediable difference produces a longing in the Self for possession that, frustrated, turns into violent aggression against the impenetrable Other.

The origin of the philosophical conception of a Self defined by lack, by an unquenchable desire to recover a wholeness that he has lost ever-projected onto an Other as locus of that lost paradise, is in Plato's *The Symposium*. There Aristophanes tells a fable about men as originally composite self-contained beings, whole unto themselves, whose arrogance Zeus punished by splitting them into two halves condemned to forever seek a reunion with the lost half of their being.[3]

Hegel conceived the irremediable opposition of Self and Other in terms of the relation of Master to Slave. The individual for Hegel is dependent on the Other's recognition, and mastery over the Other involves winning his recognition by force. The slave capitulates to the master's will, recognizing him as master. For Hegel, desire is born of the consciousness of lack, and the Self's attempt to fulfill his ontological desires leads him to an aggressive, destructive appropriation or "negation" of the object of his desire.

For Sartre as well, the Self/Other relation is marked by the aggressive will of the Self to absorb, assimilate, 'cannibalize' the Other. As Douglas Kirsner notes, in Sartre's *Being and Nothingness,*

> [a]ll human relationships are of a mutually devouring kind—one's being is swallowed up by or absorbed by another and vice versa . . . According to Sartre the self, as a nothingness, is so empty, so inherently deprived of satisfactory fulfillment that he feels he needs to be certain

3. Plato, *The Symposium,* 58–65.

of the Other—which he cannot be by the nature of the Other's separateness and subjectivity. This leads to a sadistic drive to incorporate or absorb the Other with the concomitant fear of destroying the very person he desires.[4]

Sartre's vision of sadistic violence produced by the Self's impotent ontological desire to absorb the Other had a great impact on Latin American literature beginning in the 1950s and 1960s, when Saer was starting his career as a writer. The Argentine Julio Cortázar expresses it through his tortured, ontologically insecure protagonist Horacio Oliveira in *Rayuela* (*Hopscotch*), a 1963 novel that strongly influenced writers of Saer's generation:

> How we all hate each other, without realizing that affection is the present guise of that hatred, and how the reason for such profound hatred is this unbridgeable space between you and I, between this and that. All tenderness is an ontological clawing, you see, an attempt to grab hold of the ungraspable.[5]

In a short story entitled "The Smallest Woman in the World," the Brazilian Clarice Lispector puts the aggressive impulses of the Self toward the Other in anthropological terms, using cannibalism as a metaphor for the devouring nature of the Self/Other relation. The story is about the French explorer Marcel Pretre's discovery in the remote jungles of Africa of the smallest human beings in the world—a tribe of pygmies—and among them of the smallest woman in the world, whom he names Little Flower. The explorer, awed by his discovery, begins to collect data about these tiny, rare beings. Along with the usual stereotypical ethnographic details—the women cook maize, grind cassava root, and collect vegetables while the men hunt; their language is "short and simple, consisting only of the essentials"; they dance to the beat of a primitive drum—the explorer finds that they live in fear of being captured and devoured by the cannibalistic *bantos*.[6] The threat of cannibalistic absorption becomes in Lispector's story a metaphor for the predatory nature of the Self's attraction to the Other, and for anthropology as a cannibalistic discourse.

4. Douglas Kirsner, "Sartre and the Collective Neurosis of Our Time," 218.

5. Julio Cortázar, *Rayuela,* 557.

6. Clarice Lispector, "The Smallest Woman in the World," in *Family Ties,* 90. This is a translation of Lispector's "A menor mulher do mundo" from *Laços de família.* Subsequent references to the translation will be made in the text.

The public's reaction to the appearance of Little Flower's picture in the Sunday paper reveals the dark side of the French explorer's tender awe before the object of his study. The subliminally tyrannical nature of emotions like tenderness and pity experienced by those who see Little Flower's picture is underscored by Lispector's irony: "In another apartment, a woman felt such a perverse tenderness for the daintiness of the African woman that . . . Little Flower should never be left alone with the tenderness of that woman. Who knows to what darkness of love her affection might extend" (90). Little Flower's picture unnerves this woman, who spends the day troubled, "overcome . . . by desire" (91). In another house an entire family is overcome by the same "nostalgia": "In the heart of each member of the family there arose the gnawing desire to possess that minute and indomitable thing which had been saved from being devoured . . ." (92). Little Flower rejects this kind of predatory tenderness that objectifies and takes possession of her. Disarming the intent explorer, the smallest woman in the world, celebrating her continued freedom from the devouring *bantos,* laughs out loud in a spontaneous outburst of joy that "the uncomfortable explorer did not succeed in classifying" (94).

Like Lispector, Saer associates the anthropological impulse with a cannibalistic ingestion of the Other in *The Witness.* The novel recreates the legendary ill-fated arrival of the Spaniard Juan Díaz de Solís's expedition to Río de la Plata in the sixteenth century. According to historical accounts, Solís and some of his men, having disembarked on American soil, were set upon, killed, and devoured by the cannibalistic natives while their companions remaining on board the ships watched in horror. Among the men who accompanied Solís on his fatal mission into alien territory, there is said to have been one Francisco del Puerto, who was spared by the Indians and lived among them for the next ten years.[7] In *The Witness* Saer invents the apocryphal memoirs of this survivor singled out by fate.

By the time the narrator sits down to write years after his return to Spain, the *colastiné* Indians (one of various historical tribes inhabiting the islands of the Paraná River at the time of the Conquest) have long been wiped out, the victims of genocide. The narrator writes, impelled by the conviction that the Indians, somehow sensing their fate, "wanted there to be a witness

---

7. María Luisa Bastos outlines this history in "Eficacias del verosímil no realista: dos novelas recientes de Juan José Saer," 3–4.

to and a survivor of their passage through this material mirage; they wanted someone to tell their story" (querían que de su pasaje por ese espejismo material quedase, ante el mundo, su narrador).[8] Yet the narrator suppresses the fact that when the *colastiné* finally send him off in a boat to be found by his fellow countrymen, he himself provokes the genocidal attack on them by betraying their location and habits to the Spanish. His betrayal seals the fate of the tribe, and triggers his compulsion, years later as an old man, to resurrect them by writing an ethnographic account, a version of salvage ethnography.

The narrator's complicity in the Indians' tragic end suggests that their murder is necessary for him to cannibalistically feed off the dead, producing a document that at once resurrects and entombs the native Other in writing. This relation between genocide and narrative recalls Hegel's view that since language kills what it names, annihilates the real in order to take its place, then symbolic systems are therefore founded on murder. Language traitorously usurps, betrays the real, and replaces it with a system of signs.

For Jacques Lacan, the Self's fall from wholeness to separation is a fall into language. Language in Lacan's view is structured by the recognition of lack and the illusion of mastering the world outside the Self by naming it, capturing it.[9] Since language cannot ever conjure what the Self desires as presence, can only allude to its inexorable absence, the nature of language is to be elegiac, nostalgic, erotic: an expression of the Self's impossible desire to possess the inaccessible Other. All writing is "anthropological," then, as it struggles to take possession of an Other it can never grasp.

This relation between desire, language, and the anthropological imagination is suggested in Miguel Angel Asturias's *Men of Maize*. In the 1949 novel the figure of the *tecuna,* the legendary Woman who vanishes from her husband's house never to be seen again, becomes a metaphor for the ever-vanishing object of the Self's desire: erotic desire stands for ontological desire. The story of the *tecuna* in *Men of Maize* is a folkloric version of the philosophical tradition that posits the Self as an incomplete being ever straining toward union with his lost complement. The priest Father Valentín's anthropological writings about the *tecuna* folklore become yet

8. Juan José Saer, *The Witness,* 144. This is a translation from Saer's *El entenado* (1983), 134. Subsequent page references in the text will refer first to the translation and then to the original.

9. For a general overview of the influence of psychoanalytic theory and Lacan on Argentine literary criticism, see Nicolás Rosa, "La crítica literaria contemporánea."

another version of the Self's attempt to grasp the elusive Other, taking possession through writing.

In *Men of Maize* the time of the Self's perfect oneness with the world can only exist outside the space of the novel, before the Conquest sets in motion the process that provokes the rift between the Indian Self and the world he inhabits, before language alienates the Self from the real. In modern primitivism, as in Asturias's novel, the West fantasizes the "primitive" Other as being closer to an original oneness denied to the modern Self in his inexorable separation. The primitive becomes a figure of desire that like the *tecuna* haunts the imagination of modern man. Ethnologists like Emile Durkheim and Lucien Lévy-Bruhl envisioned primitive tribal man as living in a world of social harmony, at one with the earth and free from the plague of modern man's alienation from collective forms of life. For Durkheim, primitive ritual reinforced the collective bond and the religious faith of primitive societies. In Saer's novel, however, the West's fantasy of the Other's plenitude is demythified, for the primitive Other the narrator encounters is, as it turns out, as deficient, as cursed by lack, as the European Self.

The Indians with whom the narrator of *The Witness* spends ten years of his life are beings marked by lack: "They sensed a lack they could not name; they were seeking without knowing what they sought or what they had lost" (Que algo les faltaba era seguro . . . Parecían presentir la falta de algo sin llegar a nombrarlo; como si buscaran sin saber qué buscaban ni qué se les había perdido, 78–79; 75). Their ritual cannibalism and its orgiastic aftermath come to represent for the narrator not the key to collective solidarity and the reaffirmation of faith of Durkheim's primitives, but rather a repeated, anguished attempt to restore a lost plenitude, to return to a state of unity beyond the world of "fallen, ephemeral fragments" (fragmentos perdidos y pasajeros, 43; 43).[10] Rather than strengthen collective bonds, the tribe's ritual only serves to sink them, as isolated individuals, deeper into a profoundly solipsistic alienation.

The Indians' aggressive, cannibalistic will to conquer and possess (ingest) the Other becomes a mirror image in the novel of the conquistadors'

10. That the urge to cannibalize is precipitated by a feeling of loss and separation is suggested by Freud, for whom cannibalism "appears to be at the very basis of the concept of self and other, which occurs when the symbiotic relationship between mother and child, of eater and eaten becomes divided." See Maggie Kilgour, *From Communion to Cannibalism: An Anatomy of Metaphors of Incorporation,* 12.

impulse to conquer and colonize, propelled by impotence, lack, and desire. In this contrast to Durkheim's romanticized primitive, Saer's novel follows the revisionist thought begun by Bataille and the "dissident surrealists" who posited "the essential identity of primitive and modern man."[11]

Walter Mignolo has noted that cannibalism was "one of the most significant trademarks . . . in the construction of the image of the Amerindians during the sixteenth and early seventeenth centuries."[12] From the time of the original encounter between Europeans and indigenous populations of America, the anthropological imagination has been haunted by the specter of cannibalism and sacrificial violence. In the sixteenth century, that the natives were eaters of human flesh was a sign of their absolute Otherness. Cannibalism was considered a savage practice that had nothing to do with "civilized" man.[13] Nevertheless, the West's fascination for cannibalistic and sacrificial practices is evident in the persistent return of anthropology to the theme in nineteenth- and twentieth-century studies of primitive religion.

Studies of primitive religion undertaken by thinkers like Frazer, Durkheim, Lévy-Bruhl, Mauss, Freud, Bataille, and Girard betray a "nostalgia for the religious experience" on the part of a society whose positivistic assumptions presumed a lack of faith in spiritual matters.[14] The waning of positivism in the beginning of the twentieth century was due to a growing sense that mankind was diminished and floundering without religious faith, and that irrational forces unrecognized by positivism played a significant role in human behavior. Anthropologists looked to primitive societies for a model of collective life ruled by faith, immersed in a vital religious tradition, and in touch with a sacred realm that the West had lost sight of somewhere along the way. In particular, the primitive's ritual practices were seen as expressions of vitality, group solidarity, and communion with the sacred. Durkheim viewed the intensity of ritual as lifting the individual outside himself in a paroxysm of communion and transcendence, an anthropological

---

11. Letvin, *Sacrifice in the Surrealist Novel,* 39.

12. Mignolo, "When Speaking Was Not Good Enough: Illiterates, Barbarians, Savages, and Cannibals," 312.

13. In his essay "On cannibals," Montaigne skeptically attempted to undermine this extreme but pervasive view by problematizing "civilized" man's claim to lead a superior, less barbaric lifestyle. Montaigne chided his contemporaries by noting "that we all call barbarous anything that is contrary to our own habits." Montaigne argued that cannibalism was in some sense natural, had a logic intrinsic to the organic nature of life and death, in contrast to torture, a barbaric abomination practiced by Europeans. In Montaigne, *Essays,* 108.

14. Letvin, *Sacrifice in the Surrealist Novel,* 15.

vision that corresponds to the surrealists' desire to experience exalted states of being.

A desire to restore to modern man the primitive's intimate relation to the sacred underlies the Collège de Sociologie's conception of a "sacred sociology." The founders of the Collège—Bataille, Michel Leiris, and Roger Caillois—were especially drawn to the paroxysm experienced in ritual acts of violence such as sacrifice. Bataille linked violent, erotic, and ritual acts as transgressive attempts to transcend the limits of the human condition: "Without a doubt these limits are necessary to man, but he cannot for all that endure them. It is in transgressing these limits . . . that man affirms his essence." In contrast to modern man, Bataille's primitive knows the horror of life because he lives it intimately from day to day. For Bataille, civilized man's recoil in the face of violence, death, and putrefaction conceals his ambivalence, his subliminal attraction to states of convulsion that prefigure the passing from the known parameters of life into the unknown realm of death: "the extreme fear of decay and bloody mutilations is tied to a violent attraction that we all would prefer to conceal."[15]

The desire to experience the impenetrable beyond in liminal acts of eroticism, violence, and ritual—experiences that threaten to erase the boundaries of Self and Other—leads back to the primitive, whose orgiastic, sacrificial, cannibalistic rites become signs of an ontological quest. The Western observer can no longer situate himself on the outside, surreptitiously peering in at these savage primitives, but must acknowledge his intimate involvement with them. Despite his initial repulsion, the narrator of *The Witness* admits that the roasting flesh of the unfortunate Spaniards on the Indians' fire provokes in him a repressed desire: "almost against my will, however hard I tried to swallow my saliva, something else, something stronger than repugnance or fear, persisted in making my mouth water" (algo más fuerte que la repugnancia y el miedo se obstinaba, casi contra mi voluntad, a que ante el espectáculo que estaba contemplando en la luz cenital se me hiciera agua a la boca, 45; 45–46). The captive's residual appetite for the Indians' cannibalistic feast confirms Bataille's sense that "that which most violently revolts us is within us."[16]

15. Cited in Letvin, *Sacrifice in the Surrealist Novel,* 44, 40.
16. Cited in Letvin, *Sacrifice in the Surrealist Novel,* 45. The motif of ritual, sacrificial violence—a constant in Saer's works—is especially evident in *El limonero real* (1974) and *Nadie nada nunca* (1980), as is his debt to Bataille.

As *entenado,* the nameless narrator of *The Witness* is son and not son, being (ente-) and nothingness (nada/o).[17] He is caught between two worlds, the Spanish and the *colastiné,* and both he and the members of the *colastiné* tribe suffer from the same sense of the fragility, of the unreality, of their marginal condition. In his narrative, the former captive emphasizes the universality of the human condition as one of captivity and isolation (as in Sartre's existentialism) and its effect on both himself and his captors. He refers to himself as "the abandoned one," he who was left behind; but the *colastiné* are also "abandoned and naked selves" (criaturas abandonadas y desnudas, 87; 83). He describes himself as well as the *colastiné* using images of being adrift, of shipwreck, of being on a voyage fraught with peril toward an unidentified destination: "The current carried me steadily on until evening" (La corriente me iba llevando, firme, en el atardecer, 94; 89); "the tribe was embarked on some endless inner journey" (la tribu estaba embarcada en un viaje sin fondo . . . , 62; 61); "I drifted lost and alone" (yo derivaba, perdido y abandonado, 94; 90); "they were like a raft of shipwrecked sailors as a storm rages in the dead of night" (eran como náufragos . . . mientras golpea la tormenta, 88; 84).[18] The narrator describes the anguished torment he perceives in the Indians' eyes as similar to that which overcomes the Spanish captain of the ill-fated expedition in a premonition of his own imminent death, when his gaze becomes "simultaneously intense and vague" (encendida y vaga al mismo tiempo, 21; 22): "it is the presence of that inexpressible something in their eyes . . . I think there must be the same look in the eyes of the man being sucked into the slimy pit . . . ." (Los ojos de los indios traicionaban siempre esa presencia inenarrable . . . los ojos de un hombre atrapado en un abismo viscoso, no deben mirar de otra manera, 92; 87). The narrator finds his own captivity to be a mirror image of the tribe's existence "imprisoned within themselves" (en la cárcel de los cuerpos, 55; 54).

The narrator comes to view the Indians' cannibalistic impulse that lies dormant until it erupts at a given time yearly, during which the ritual repeats

17. Margaret Jull Costa's translation of *El entenado* as *The Witness* aptly underscores the primacy of existential philosophy in the novel, but is not a literal translation. The literal translation of *entenado* is "stepson."

18. The recurring image of being adrift suggests an allusion to Lacan's notion of "the 'drifting' moment of desire": "*dérive,* which corresponds to adrift, in the sense of something adrift, being dragged by currents and not knowing where it is going." Bice Benvenuto and Roger Kennedy, *The Works of Jacques Lacan: An Introduction,* 173.

itself inexorably, as the expression of an invisible force acting through the Indians against their will—"a very ancient sound" (un rumor arcaico, 53; 53), "some arbitrary power ruling them from the blackness" (una presencia que los gobernaba a pesar de ellos, 67; 65–66), "[t]he ubiquitous fire that consumed them" ([e]sa intemperie que los maltrataba, 87; 83). The existence of an impersonal force that imposes certain structures on human behavior, that makes each "tribe" an individual variation on a submerged, unalterable pattern, assures that "[e]very action, however insignificant, was part of a pre-established order" ([t]odo acto, por mínimo que fuese, entraba en un orden preestablecido, 141; 131). Like leaves tossed by the wind, the *colastiné* are driven by the same forces that govern natural cycles: "Tossed on the incandescent breath of that fire they were no more masters of their actions than the dust whirled up by a November storm" (Llevados y traídos por ese hálito incandescente, no eran más dueños de sus actos que la espiral de tierra en el ciclón de noviembre, 87–88; 83).

In a children's game that the narrator witnesses again and again over the ten years he spends with the *colastiné,* the figure of a spiral comes to represent for him a model for the repetitive nature of human activity beyond all contingency, for while the individual children, the actors, change constantly, the game itself is invariable. The narrator speculates that the repetition of the game has a meaning that goes beyond itself, for its persistent recurrence in his memory suggests the playing out of a hidden intention:

> I do not know why but I imagine I can see in this memory, which grows clearer with the years, some obscure sign from the world surfacing to the light of day. Perhaps it is because I find it hard to accept that the game's persistence through many generations of children and its insistent presence in my memory should be mere chance and have no significance whatsoever when measured against infinity. Such determination to endure in the unfriendly light of the world suggests, perhaps, some complicity with its deepest essence. (149)

> (En sus rasgos, que año tras año se van precisando, me parece entrever que algún signo oscuro del mundo se presenta, quién sabe por qué causa, a la luz del día, ya que es difícil imaginar que la persistencia de ese acto por parte de los niños, a través de muchas generaciones, y su presencia insistente en mi memoria, sean simples hechos casuales que, medidos con la vara del infinito, no tengan ninguna significación.) (138)

The narrator's perception of a "rhythm," a "presence," a "sound" that manipulates the Indians "with its own peculiar and excessive rigour" (con un rigor propio y sin medida, 88; 84) recalls Lévi-Strauss's structuralist vision of a "master-meaning," of "certain eternal truths" inscribed in nature that determine the pattern of natural landscapes as well as of human actions and cultural productions: "the most majestic meaning of all is surely that which precedes, and commands, and, to a large extent, explains the others." The presence of a "master-meaning" controlling and channeling all human endeavor reinforces the "essential identity of primitive and modern man," for according to Lévi-Strauss, "human societies . . . never create absolutely, but merely choose certain combinations from an ideal repertoire."[19] The Indians are driven by hidden structures and the implacable will of an inscrutable force; nevertheless, Saer's "postmodern" sensibility makes him suspicious of Lévi-Strauss's pretension to uncover or identify the "key" to such a "master-meaning":

> To the positivist idea that everything is structure, we might add that the fact that these structures exist is also mysterious . . . The final conclusion is always a confession of failure: our tools for understanding the world are more elaborate every day but the world stubbornly remains incomprehensible.[20]

Lévi-Strauss's "master-meaning" that controls the variation and combination of a given set of elements suggests the arbitrariness, the fragility of the individual's identification with a particular culture, a region, or a nation. Horacio Oliveira in *Hopscotch* detects the expression of a universal substratum in human experience indifferent to national boundaries in jazz:

> something completely indifferent to national rituals, to inviolable traditions, to language and to folklore: a cloud without boundaries, a spy of the air and water, an archetypal form, something from way back, from below, that reconciles Mexicans, Norwegians, Russians and Spaniards, leads them back to the dark inner forgotten fire . . . [21]

In an interview, Saer expresses his conviction that the Self's identification with a particular nationality is of a contingent, arbitrary nature: "They try to

19. Lévi-Strauss, *Tristes Tropiques*, 48–49, 186. Lévi-Strauss's theory of course echoes Plato's concept of eternal Ideas or Forms.
20. Matilde Sánchez, "Saer: 'La literatura es objeto y misterio.' "
21. Cortázar, *Rayuela*, 204.

tell us that the country is an absolute, when in reality it is the contingent . . . one's place of birth, and birth itself, is a matter of chance."[22] The fragility of the Self's ties to a particular region or country or culture can be seen in the narrator of *The Witness,* who finds that "two or three years after my arrival it was as if I had never lived anywhere else" (dos o tres años después de haber llegado era como si nunca hubiese estado en otra parte, 90; 86). In his new existence among the *colastiné* the captive gives himself over to the habit and empty activities of the daily round that impose themselves on his consciousness and estrange him from his own past. He is struck by the (Sartrean) revelation: "Nothing is innate in us" (Nada nos es connatural, 90; 86), everything in us of a contingent nature is arbitrary and changeable. The captive's tale recalls certain of Borges's short stories in which protagonists' destinies involve closely identifying with, and sometimes crossing over to, the enemy camp. The narrator of "Story of the Warrior and the Captive" muses about the barbarian soldier Droctulft, "a Lombard soldier who, during the siege of Ravenna, left his companions and died defending the city he had previously attacked," and a British woman captured as a child by Araucana Indians in the *pampas* of Argentina who goes native, abandoning her former life. Borges's story underscores the arbitrariness of the Self's identification with particular symbolic systems or cultures in the face of an overarching drama that transcends the individual parts played, however passionately, by its actors: "The obverse and the reverse of this coin are, for God, the same."[23] The narrator of *The Witness* has a Borgesian sense of the prewritten drama directing human life that he expresses in judging a theatrical version of his tale that plays to enthusiastic crowds all over Europe: "Long, long ago the true meaning of our cheap parody must already have been written into some grander plot that also encompassed us" (El verdadero sentido de nuestra simulación chabacana debía estar previsto, desde siempre, en algún argumento que nos abarcara, 115; 108).

Saer has stated that *The Witness* is his most personal book.[24] Perhaps this is because the captive's precarious insertion into an alien cultural environment resonates with the experience of the exile, of "the eternal outsider" (45; 45) looking in, a detached witness to the strange rituals of others, to their "incomprehensible language" (36; 36). Despite his original feeling of detachment and disorientation among the *colastiné,* after his

---

22. Ana Basualdo, "El desierto retórico: Entrevista con Juan José Saer," 15.
23. Jorge Luis Borges, "Story of the Warrior and the Captive," 127, 131.
24. Sánchez, "Saer: 'La literatura es objeto y misterio.'"

release and return to Spain, the captive feels once again the wrenching sense of being an exile in a foreign world:

> My whole body remembers those years of intense, carnal life which seem to have penetrated it so deeply that it has grown insensible to any other experience. Just as the Indians from some of the neighbouring tribes used to trace an invisible circle in the air to protect themselves from the unknown, my body, wrapped in the skin of those years, now lets nothing in from outside. (146–47)

> (Puedo decir que, de algún modo, mi cuerpo entero recuerda, a su manera, esos años de vida espesa y carnal, y que esa vida pareciera haberlo impregnado tanto que lo hubiese vuelto insensible a cualquier otra experiencia. De la misma manera que los indios de algunas tribus vecinas trazaban en el aire un círculo invisible que los protegía de lo desconocido, mi cuerpo está como envuelto en la piel de esos años que ya no dejan pasar nada del exterior.) (136)

Although he has lived in France for more than twenty years, Saer returns again and again in his writing to the Santa Fe region of Argentina and the banks of the Paraná River, as if to confess, like the narrator in his old age about his years of captivity, "the confused glitter of that past is the only story I have to tell" (yo no tengo, aparte de ese centelleo confuso, ninguna otra cosa que contar, 147; 136). The persistence of an Argentine reality in Saer's narrative, however, does not negate his sense of the contingent nature of nationality and cultural identifications, for he insists: "The specificity of each country is indifferent to me"; "In reality, I think that setting my narratives in the same place is rather a negation of regionalism."[25]

In effect, if Argentina persists in the writer's imagination it is as the representation of a lost childhood world from which the Self has been exiled:

> we are in large part the place where we were born. The first years of a man's life are crucial for his later development. The mother's language has to do with feelings, sensations, emotions, sexuality. One's country therefore belongs to the realm of the private.[26]

The Latin American writer in exile carries this primitive, lost world within, like the Indians: "For them that place was the home of the world. If

25. Sánchez, "La literatura es objeto y misterio"; Basualdo, "El desierto retórico," 15.
26. Basualdo, "El desierto retórico," 15.

anything existed it could not do so outside of that place . . . Wherever they went, they carried it within them" (Ese lugar era, para ellos, la casa del mundo. Si algo podía existir, no podía hacerlo fuera de él . . . Dondequiera que fuesen, la llevaban adentro, 126–27; 118). At the same time, for the exile, the memory of home takes on the irreality of a dream that becomes remote and unreal after it ends, as for the narrator in the estrangement of his new existence as a captive, "the captain, my companions and the ships all seemed to me like the unconnected fragments of an ill-remembered dream" (mis compañeros, el capitán y los barcos, me parecían los restos inconexos de un sueño mal recordado, 31; 32).

The experience of exile as one of rending, of being cut off from an original wholeness ("the mother's language"), is similar to the rending experience of birth. The narrator frequently describes his condition whether as a captive or as a newly repatriated Spaniard as comparable to that of a newborn: "I was a foundling and, like a dazed and bloody babe leaving the dark night of his mother's womb, all I could do was cry" (yo nacía sin saberlo y como el niño que sale, ensangrentado y atónito, de esa noche oscura que es el vientre de su madre, no podía hacer otra cosa que echarme a llorar, 35; 35).[27] Exile, captivity, and birth in turn become metaphors for the solipsistic experience of the individual human being, that the *colastiné* as a singular tribe among myriad other tribes represents: "Each tribe lived in a singular universe, infinite and unique, which bore no relation whatsoever to that of neighbouring tribes" (Cada tribu vivía en un universo singular, infinito y único, que ni siquiera rozaba con el de las tribus vecinas, 125; 117).

The singular, impenetrable universe in which the tribe lives is suggestive of the Self as a being distinct from all others, whose perceptions, sensations, and memory of a lived past are unique and uncommunicable. The narrator's compulsion to resurrect the memory of the *colastiné* tribe in his writing is an attempt to salvage his own past from the oblivion of his imminent death, for

> [i]n this respect death and memory are identical: they are unique to each man . . . It is because of their uniqueness that each man dies, because that is what dies . . . is transient and never reborn in others . . .

27. See also for example page 43 (43) where the narrator refers to "my newborn eyes," and page 112 (105) where he speaks of "returning as I am slowly and fearlessly through successive births to the common place of origin." The narrator's references to birth suggest a Lacanian reading in which the Self is thrust into a world of signs that alienate him from himself.

the unique memories which feed the illusion of a shared rememberer whom death will ultimately erase. (157–58)

([e]n eso se revelan iguales muerte y recuerdos: en que son, para cada hombre, únicos . . . Cada hombre muere de tenerlos únicos, porque justamente lo que muere, lo que es pasajero y no renace en otros . . . son esos recuerdos únicos que alimentan el engaño de un rememorador exclusivo que la muerte acabará por borrar.) (146–47)

The narrator's attempt to capture and concretize his experience in words in order to stave off his own mortality is comparable to the tribe's anxious attempts to prevent the imminent annihilation of their world. According to the narrator, for the *colastiné* "each human action was aimed at preserving the dubious stability of a world under the continued threat of destruction" (todos los actos humanos estaban destinados a preservar, a cada momento, la constancia improbable del mundo al que acechaba, continua, la aniquilación, 141; 131–32). The precariousness of their world is inscribed as well in their language: "if they want to say 'there is a tree' . . . they say 'it seems tree'. But 'seems' has more a feeling of untrustworthiness than sameness" (si quieren decir que hay un árbol . . . dicen *parece árbol.* Pero parece tiene menos el sentido de similitud que el de desconfianza, 130; 122).

The failure of words to capture an unstable reality reflects the futility of Conquest as an act of possession. The narrator perceives this futility in the Spaniards' endeavor as they disembark on American soil: "Each time we disembarked we were like a fleeting irritation come from nowhere, an ephemeral fever that glimmered for a moment at the edge of the water and then was gone" (cada vez que desembarcábamos, éramos como un hormigueo fugaz salido de la nada, una fiebre efímera que espejeaba unos momentos al borde del agua y después se desvanecía, 22; 23). The Spaniards' attempt to possess and colonize by naming meets with the stubborn resistance of the landscape itself: "After its baptism and appropriation the dumb earth stubbornly withheld any sign or signal" (Después del bautismo y de la apropiación, esa tierra muda persistía en no dejar ningún signo, en mandar ninguna señal, 21; 23).

Like the power of domination through Conquest, the amassing of knowledge represents a will to power to wield against the threat of dispersion and annihilation. The narrator, back in Spain after ten years with the Indians for whom "the main attribute of all things was precariousness" (127; 119), finds that his beloved teacher and protector Father Quesada cannot instill in him desire or respect for the power of knowledge: "Teaching me Greek, Hebrew and science was the least of it: what he found hard was convincing me of their value and importance" (más que el latín, el griego, el hebreo y las ciencias que me enseñó, fue dificultoso inculcarme su valor y su necesidad, 105; 99).[28]

If systems of knowledge give the illusion of mastery, the act of writing involves for Saer a letting go, an experience of "shipwreck (naufragio)," of being adrift ("à la dérive"), suspended between the precarious world of the text concretized in language, and the nothingness that surrounds it, threatening to annihilate it. "To be a writer," suggests Saer, "requires a great capacity for disengagement, for uncertainty, for abandon."[29] The writer's experience of uncertainty, of giving himself over to forces beyond his conscious control, is recreated in the reader's complementary experience of the process of reading, for submitting oneself to the world of a text is a kind of captivity. The *colastiné* tribe creates a world (like an author) that is preserved/sustained only in the "re-writing" of a witness, a reader, a captive. The interdependent relation of the tribe and its captive, then, is like that of an author and his reader, on whose parasitic, cannibalistic appropriation the text's existence depends: "they felt they had constantly to make real the apparently solid world so that it did not vanish like a thread of smoke into the evening air" (a ese mundo que parecía tan sólido, había que actualizarlo a cada momento para que no desvaneciese como un hilo de humo en el atardecer, 129; 121).

The Indians' cannibalistic, orgiastic ritual becomes a metaphor for the act of writing in its desire to transcend the limits inscribed in language, to experience the ineffable beyond of words whose access is barred to the Self, is irremediably Other. *The Witness* retells the Conquest as a

---

28. Saer's critique of systems of knowledge and acts of conquest in *The Witness* makes it difficult to accept Amaryll Chanady's interpretation of the novel that she elaborates in "Saer's Fictional Representation of the Amerindian in the Context of Modern Historiography." Chanady feels that the captive's writing about the *colastiné* reflects a confident faith in the superiority of the West with respect to indigenous populations, and that the Spanish are portrayed as agents of progress who "counteract dissolution with their cultural institutions" (703–4). In fact, as I have shown, the novel negates the evolutionary notion of progression in history in its demythification of the act of conquest and systems of knowledge (which belong to the realm of the contingent) as delusions. Chanady explicitly accuses Saer of bad faith in his construction of the Indians as inferior to the Europeans, a patent misreading of the novel.

29. Cited in Jorgelina Corbatta, "Juan José Saer: Narración versus realidad," 391.

philosophical reflection on the encounter of a fragile Self with an Other who merely presents a mirror image of the Self's incompleteness. At the end of the novel, the narrator recalls a night during the final days of his ten-year captivity when he and the Indians experience an eclipse as an epiphany that confirms their cosmic pessimism:

> I'm sure that the darkness was penetrating as deeply in them as it was in me, that they no longer had left any trace of that little light that shone for them from time to time provisionally and insignificantly. Finally we were able to witness the true color of our country, bereft of its deceptive variety and without the thickness conferred on things by that fever that consumes us from the time the light dawns until we've sunk deep into the center of the night. (166)

> (Como a mí mismo, estoy seguro que esa oscuridad les estaba entrando tan hondo que ya no les quedaba, tampoco adentro, ninguna huella de la lucecita que, de tanto en tanto, provisoria y menuda, veían brillar. Al fin podíamos percibir el color justo de nuestra patria, desembarazado de la variedad engañosa y sin espesor conferida a las cosas por esa fiebre que nos consume desde que empieza a clarear y no cede hasta que no nos hemos hundido bien en el centro de la noche.) (155)

In *Historia general de las Indias,* Francisco López de Gómara relates how Columbus, in possession of the tools of Western knowledge, conquers the Indians by "predicting" an eclipse the terrified natives experience as sorcery. In Saer's version, the eclipse undoes the Conquest's (and Anthropology's) dream of knowledge and power, reveals it to be a chimera—a "fever that consumes us."

# AFTERWORD

## The Anthropological Imagination and the Question of a Latin American Postmodernism

In the anthropological imagination of Latin American writers, the Other has been a chimera, a foil in the West's ongoing narrative about itself—indeed, "a nullity . . . [that] reflects any desire," in Christopher Miller's apt formulation.[1] According to Edward Bruner, anthropologists construct stories or narratives about the Other that reflect the anthropologist's worldview rather than any intrinsic truths about the Others they represent, and these stories shift—recede or become dominant—to conform to changes in "the social context": "different narratives," he suggests, "are foregrounded in the discourse of different historical eras."[2] Following Bruner's formulation, one could say that three distinct narrative paradigms have characterized the anthropological imagination in Latin America in the twentieth century. Although these narratives have sometimes overlapped, each has been the dominant "story" told in different "social contexts."

The dominant narrative in nineteenth- and early-twentieth-century literature and anthropology stigmatized the Other's difference as an obstacle to modernizing projects of national development. The Other's resistance to the homogenization of Latin American nations according to evolutionary schemas of development was seen in this narrative as a social problem (in Ortiz, in Sarmiento), and heterogeneous, hybrid social forms were viewed negatively as corrupt, impure deviations from an inevitable desired pattern.

In the early twentieth century, this narrative was challenged along with its positivistic assumptions by a counternarrative that questioned the value of modernity's displacement of traditional ways of life. The surrealists and their distant literary heirs, the

1. Miller, *Blank Darkness,* 49.
2. Edward M. Bruner, "Ethnography as Narrative," 151, 145.

transcultural novelists, celebrated the indigenous Other's continued attachment to premodern traditions in the face of what they saw as the West's soulless drive to modernize at the expense of such traditions and their diversity.

Although the first narrative stigmatized the Other's difference with respect to modernity, the second narrative celebrated the same difference as a counterpoint to the West's spiritually empty triumphs. Both narratives set indigenous against modernizing forces in a mode of potentially tragic conflict, as in Carpentier's *The Kingdom of This World* or in the "transcultural" novels *Deep Rivers* and Augusto Roa Bastos's 1967 *Hijo de hombre* (*Son of Man*) where both sides become engaged in ritualized epic clashes that signal their fundamental incompatibility, their refusal of synthesis.

In the late twentieth century, an emerging narrative distances itself from the binary oppositions that underlie the first two narratives as it celebrates the dynamic presence in Latin America of hybrid cultural forms. Drawing its impetus and theoretical focus from contemporary discussions of postmodernism, this narrative—which I will suggest reflects a "postmodern anthropological imagination"—bears witness to the failure of modernizing projects derived from Enlightenment visions of universal perfectibility that have shown themselves to be such elusive goals in Latin America, while taking account of the myriad, hybrid, scattered populations and subjectivities that have resisted incorporation in models of national identity based on a universalizing synthesis. Norbert Lechner articulates the double movement of this narrative's acknowledgment of the centrifugal tendencies of indigenous resistance, and its "disenchantment" with utopian projections of synthesis, in the following way:

> Disenchantment always has two faces: the loss of an illusion and, for that very reason, a resignification of reality. The constructive dimension of the current disenchantment resides in the *praise of heterogeneity*. We are in the presence of a new dynamic. . . . For too many years, we have denounced the "structural heterogeneity" of Latin America as an obstacle to development, without considering that it could foment a much more dense and rich interaction than the desired homogenization.[3]

Santiago Colás associates the drive to synthesize with Latin American modernity, contrasting it to the postmodern attitude: the "inability to acknowledge and to live with contradiction, this intolerance for impurity, this

3. Norbert Lechner, "A Disenchantment Called Postmodernism," 128–29.

radical utopian impulse, more than anything else, marks Latin American modernity. And, more than anything, the realization that such impurities are not only inevitable but can also be fruitful marks the Latin American postmodern."[4]

The "constructive" (Lechner) and "fruitful" (Colás) turn from modernist absolutes to postmodern impurities has implications for the construction of the Other as pure origin in the anthropological imagination of primitivist writers, who essentialized the native as an innocent living in a primal, uncorrupted world outside time. The impossible desire to perpetuate or return to such a state is thematized in modern novels like Asturias's *Men of Maize* and Carpentier's *The Lost Steps*. This novelistic return to the indigenous as the site of an original purity before the corruption of modern civilization is parodied in postmodern novels like Mario Vargas Llosa's 1987 *El hablador* (*The Storyteller*) as it is problematized in Saer's *The Witness*.

In *The Storyteller* the anthropologist Saul Zuratas "goes native," attempting like Carpentier's narrator in *The Lost Steps* to renounce the course of progressive time on which Enlightenment discourses of modernity are founded. For the narrator of *The Storyteller,* Saul's quixotic insistence on keeping the Amazon Machiguenga tribe pure is ludicrous, for his own presence among them is a sign of the loss of purity and autonomy he condemns. Saul's attempt to renew himself through a culture so evidently not his own (he is a Jew) parallels as it parodies Latin American writers' desire to find the key to their identity in remote indigenous sources rather than contemporary hybrid populations. The indigenous past, the novel suggests, is irrevocably past and beyond recovery. The product of Saul's deluded quest to become a native storyteller is a hybrid narrative marked by the interpenetration of styles as pastiche rather than a pure native story. For Vargas Llosa, an anthropology that doesn't take into account Latin America's fundamental heterogeneity remains a utopian discourse that ignores the actual social conditions in which descendants of indigenous societies live their lives.[5]

The postmodern anthropological imagination rejects the binary logic of the first two narratives—the positivist and the primitivist—wherein tradition and modernity are seen as conflicting, adversarial terms. Antonio Benítez-Rojo points to "what lies at the heart of postmodern literary analysis: a

4. Santiago Colás, *Postmodernity in Latin America: The Argentine Paradigm,* 27.

5. For an extended discussion of Vargas Llosa's "disenchantment" with the (modernist) utopian strain in his early work, see M. Keith Booker, *Vargas Llosa among the Postmodernists.*

questioning of the concept of 'unity' and a dismantling, or rather unmasking, of the mechanism that we know as 'binary opposition'—the thing that sustains, to a greater or lesser degree, the philosophical and ideological edifice of modernity."[6]

As an alternative to conceptualizing Caribbean history as the struggle between opposing forces, the hegemonic and the powerless, Benítez-Rojo offers his version of Caribbean-ness as the counterpoint of two tendencies that refuse synthesis, that can never coalesce as a unity but rather find their identity in their perpetual unresolvable counterpoint. For Benítez-Rojo, the Caribbean as a postmodern entity always in motion, in process, cannot be the holistic, self-contained passive object of knowledge that anthropology once sought, for "within postmodernity there cannot be any single truth, but instead there are many practical and momentary ones, truths without beginnings or ends, local truths, displaced truths, provisional and peremptory truths of a pragmatic nature."[7]

The resistance to a priori absolute truths and "grand narratives" that characterizes the postmodern sensibility signals a crisis of faith in discourses of modernity such as anthropology, a scientific discourse that shared in the Enlightenment's covert alignment of knowledge and power. The postmodern anthropological imagination renounces the Self's mastery over the Other by renouncing the hierarchical nature of authorial control implicit in ethnographic knowledge. James Clifford suggests that "[m]uch of our knowledge about other cultures must now be seen as contingent, the problematic outcome of intersubjective dialogue, translation, and projection."[8]

If in previous narratives the Other was set apart from the Self—was denied, in Johannes Fabian's formulation, "coevalness" with the subject of knowledge—the current shift in narrative paradigms turns the focus of the ethnographic eye away from the Other as a being set apart in time and space from the modern world toward an Other who is in all ways "coeval" with the Self. Michael M. J. Fischer notes that "one of the things the postmodern is about is the juxtaposition of things, events, and experiences once separated by time and space." Néstor García Canclini confirms the relevance of this postmodern experience for Latin America: "we live in a

6. Antonio Benítez-Rojo, *The Repeating Island: The Caribbean and the Postmodern Perspective,* 154.

7. Benítez-Rojo, *The Repeating Island,* 151.

8. Clifford and Marcus, eds., *Writing Culture,* 109.

postmodern era, a time of *bricolage* when various epochs and cultures converge that before remained apart from each other."[9]

The simultaneity of diverse elements combined in a nonhierarchical fashion that the postmodern narrative of hybridity constructs as its model, recalls the paradigmatic avant-garde genre of collage. For Nelly Richard, Latin American societies by virtue of their historical situation embody the hybridity that characterizes collage: "by an amalgamation of signs, by means of historical/cultural grafts and transplants of disjunctive codes, the Latin American mosaic prefigured postmodernist collage."[10]

As we have seen, the postmodern construction of a hybrid social space on the metaphor of collage is prefigured as well in Carpentier's 1933 novel *¡Ecué-Yamba-O!* Carpentier wasn't ready to celebrate the urban experience, as it imperiled for him the possibility for the creation of an authentic Latin American identity. But although he hesitated between a vision of the black Other as mimetic clown and as creative *bricoleur,* the disordered heterogeneity of the Latin American landscape represented as collage in *¡Ecué-Yamba-O!* reflects a social reality that resists synthesis and progression in a way that anticipates the postmodern attitude.

The destabilization of hierarchies in collage, as well as the renunciation of an authorial perspective that would make its various elements cohere in a totalizing intentionality, reflects an erosion of the Author/Self's position of dominance and authority—a ceding of mastery in formal fragmentation. For Edward Said, this crisis of mastery can be seen as well in the narratives of modernist writers like E. M. Forster, Malraux, Eliot, Mann, Lawrence, and others, for whom the fracture of the imperial domain led to the increasingly disturbing tendency of cultural Others to resist subjugation: "[t]he subaltern and the constitutively different suddenly achieved disruptive articulation exactly where in European culture silence and compliance could previously be depended on to quiet them down."[11]

Hal Foster suggests that the ambivalence of the Self/Other relation provokes a crisis in the white male subject that can be discerned in the fantasies of masculinist mastery that characterize modernist primitivism. In Foster's analysis, the primitive Other is both threatening and seductive

---

9. Fabian, *Time and the Other.* Michael M. J. Fischer, "Autobiographical Voices (1, 2, 3) and Mosaic Memory: Experimental Sondages in the (Post)modern World," 81. Néstor García Canclini, "Los estudios culturales de los 80 a los 90: perspectivas antropológicas y sociológicas en América Latina," 132.

10. Nelly Richard, "Latinoamérica y la Posmodernidad," 216.

11. Edward Said, "Representing the Colonized: Anthropology's Interlocutors," 223.

to the white male heterosexual subject because of its association with instinctual impulses that the modern subject is bound to repress and sublimate in the process of civilization that liberates him from his primitive, unsublimated drives. In the "'primitive' scenes" of Picasso, Gauguin, and others, mastery over the Other is asserted by depicting "racial, sexual, and social others in anal molds and bestial poses" that "reduce women to nature in a pictorial act of gender subjugation" or paint them as (black) prostitutes while conflating images of women and natives. For Foster, the aggression that marks avant-garde painting of "primitives" and women suggests not "a pure expression of masculinist mastery," but rather a "compensatory fantasy that bespeaks a feared *lack* of this mastery."[12] Foster underlines the ambivalence of the white male subject's desire for control and surrender, and suggests that this conflict leads to a relation with the Other that combines elements of sadism (the desire for active mastery) and masochism (the desire to passively surrender).

Foster's reading of the conflict between a desire to control and a desire to surrender in modernist primitivism brings us back to the sadomasochistic strains of Arguedas's narrative world, where conflated images of women and Indians in abject positions of powerlessness draw inexorably the sadistic attentions of a white male subject in crisis. We have seen that the dynamics of Arguedas's conflictive attraction/repulsion to the Indian Other is alternately marked by the desire for intimacy in the purity of ritual and the dread of contamination in the disorder of dirt. Foster reads Picasso's ambivalence toward an encounter with the Other he both dreaded and desired in the painter's confession about his unsettling visit to the Trocadéro Museum in Paris: "When I went to the old Trocadéro, it was disgusting. The Flea Market. The smell. I was all alone. I wanted to get away. But I didn't leave. I stayed. I stayed." Picasso's experience of "the potency of disorder and dirt" at the Trocadéro echoes the unseemly mix of pleasure and terror experienced by Arguedas's child narrator in *Deep Rivers* at the scene of the dark, dank *chichería* inhabited by women and natives: "I felt a violent desire to go out into the street . . . I couldn't feel at home . . . I would have to leave."[13]

The crisis of the white male subject in modernism that Said and Foster describe is played out as well in Darcy Ribeiro's *Maíra*, where the anthropologist's passionate desire for intimacy with the Other is shown

---

12. Hal Foster, "'Primitive' Scenes," 79.
13. Foster, "'Primitive' Scenes," 91; Arguedas, *Deep Rivers,* 169–70.

to be fraught with peril. The Other's difference in *Maíra* represents an absolute ontological divide, and the crossing of this inviolable border is a transgression fervently desired but impossible to attain. The primitivist sublime is marked by the longing for an unknowable beyond, for an impossible purity before contamination—a space where the Other resides and that cannot be penetrated without the liminal crossing into death: the penalty for miscegenation *is death,* as it is for Alma. The anthropologist's experience of the sublime as an impenetrable threshold leads to a questioning of anthropological discourse in its drive for mastery that reverberates in the epistemological crisis at the heart of the novel.

Ribeiro's fantasizing of the Other's plenitude in opposition to the Self's lack is a modernist trope that has its origins, according to Robert Young, in

> the Romantic questioning of the dominant Enlightenment ethos of civilization, progress, perfectibility . . . that saw contemporary civilization as fallen and diseased, and looked for a return to a more natural, healthy way of life . . . natural language rather than artificial rhetoric, and popular culture rather than the high culture of civilization . . . ethnicity, associated with the purity of a people, language and folk-art still in intimate relation with the soil from which they sprang.[14]

Miguel Barnet's primitivistic portrait of the runaway black slave Esteban Montejo as a creature of nature "in intimate relation to the soil" who speaks a natural language of pure poetry devoid of rhetorical artifice places him squarely in the Romantic tradition that Young describes.

According to Steven Webster, we must combat the tendency to see indigenous communities "abstractly in the Romantic tradition as 'a whole way of life' somehow unique, integral, harmonious, and Other than that supposedly led by European societies." Instead, he argues, "we need to scrutinise social action at the level of historically specific conflicts rather than abstract or suprahistorical confrontation." George Yúdice has observed that a certain postmodernism tends to fetishize Latin America as the locus for a heterogeneous, carnivalesque Otherness, thus retaining the "suprahistorical" mystifications of the primitivist sublime. In a similar vein, Paul Rabinow cautions that anthropology cannot allow itself to be seduced by aestheticizing narratives of hybridity that evade the specificity of actual social conditions. Finally, Edward Said calls on

---

14. Robert J. C. Young, *Colonial Desire: Hybridity in Theory, Culture and Race,* 42.

anthropologists "to see Others not as ontologically given but as historically constituted."[15]

The postmodern anthropological imagination in Latin America demystifies the primitivist sublime in works such as *Maíra, Biography of a Runaway Slave,* and *Deep Rivers* by inscribing the Self/Other dynamic in the realm of the social, where hybridity "is the *product* of a historical situation" and "embodies a *specific* social relation . . . wherein improvisation is not merely a formal literary reflex but a function of living in the world."[16] Contemporary genres that enact the local "improvisations" of Latin American cultural life and have been called postmodern include the *historia,* the *crónica,* and the *testimonio.* All are "anthropological" in that they focus on the dynamics of collective social groups, but in them the object of anthropological interest has shifted from the "pure" native to marginalized or hybrid urban populations and the alternative histories they represent.

Santiago Colás contrasts the "resistant, Latin American postmodernist *historia* . . . shaped by the multiple repressed and forgotten . . . subaltern histories of the everyday" to the official, imposed versions of history they unravel.[17] Carlos Alonso discusses this unraveling with respect to Latin America's grand narratives of continental unity symbolized in the mythic figure of Bolívar in Gabriel García Márquez's *The General in His Labyrinth.* In the novel, Bolívar's utopian illusion of a unified Latin American continent based on Enlightenment projections of progress and perfectibility dies a slow, agonizing death along with the hero, who, as a figure for utopian absolutes in García Márquez's imaginative historical recreation, had already become an anachronistic, walking absurdity in his own time. For Alonso, the novel is "a postmodern version of Bolívar's myth of continental consolidation" as it dramatizes with the decrepit figure of the dying general the failure of Latin American modernity "as an imperative and universal project," while suggesting the need for Latin Americans to stop mourning for what could never have been, "so that the phantom of the lost object of modernity may cease to rule the libidinal economy of Spanish American cultural discourse and social life."[18]

15. Steven Webster, "Postmodernist Theory and the Sublimation of Maori Culture," 226, 233. Yúdice, "*Testimonio* and Postmodernism," 22–23. Rabinow, "Representations Are Social Facts." Said, "Representing the Colonized," 225.

16. Sangari, "The Politics of the Possible," 160.

17. Colás, *Postmodernity in Latin America,* 126–27.

18. Carlos Alonso, "The Mourning After: García Márquez, Fuentes and the Meaning of Postmodernity in Spanish America," 260.

The *crónica,* like the *historia,* rewrites history from the point of view of the heterogeneous elements of Latin American culture that resist incorporation in a "synthesizing allegory."[19] In their "refusal to totalize," *crónicas* such as Gregorio Martínez's *Crónica de músicos y diablos* (Chronicle of musicians and devils, 1991) and Edgardo Rodríguez Juliá's *El entierro de Cortijo* (Cortijo's burial, 1983), as well as Elena Poniatowska's chronicles of the subaltern classes as an Other culture living on the margins of contemporary Mexico, challenge static, essentialist constructions of culture as a coherent, unified entity with a single voice and a single history. According to Jean Franco, in *Cortijo's Burial* Rodríguez Juliá represents Puerto Rican culture as a pastiche text of "unreconcilable patterns" that reflect "the impossibility of the typical . . . except as the sum of idiosyncracies."[20] Juan Flores praises Rodríguez Juliá's "relational, non-essentialist presentation of Puerto Rican culture in its contemporary dynamic" marked by polyvocality and the dramatization of "the multiple intersections that actually characterize the culture at any given point in time and place."[21]

Some critics have claimed that the *testimonio,* like the *historia* and the *crónica,* can be considered a postmodern genre. George Yúdice and John Beverley have judged the *testimonio* to be a practice that like the new democratic grassroots social movements in Latin America poses a challenge to political systems whose hegemony is based on the repression of heterogeneity. The Other's voice in *testimonio* becomes a mark of dissonance and polyphony that undercuts any totalitarian regime's attempts to suppress it.

Although this reading of *testimonio* is compelling and sometimes true, narratives that are counterhegemonic are not necessarily postmodern. Some *testimonios* by guerrilla writers, for example, are patently counterhegemonic, but their works are marked by the kind of absolutist discourse that Colás identifies with modernist narratives and that the postmodern militates against. Since the guerrilla writers of *testimonio* want to replace one political regime with another, their texts are single-voiced rather than polyphonic, centripetal rather than centrifugal in intention. According to

19. According to Stephen A. Tyler, anthropologists "confirm in our ethnographies our consciousness of the fragmentary nature of the postmodern world, for nothing so well defines our world as the absence of a synthesizing allegory." In "Post-Modern Ethnography: From Document of the Occult to Occult Document," 132.

20. Jean Franco, "The Nation as Imagined Community," 212, 211. See Poniatowska's *Fuerte es el silencio* (Silence is strong) for an example of her chronicles of the subaltern.

21. Juan Flores, "Cortijo's Revenge: New Mappings of Puerto Rican Culture," 194.

Juan Duchesne Winter, Che Guevara's *Diary,* a paradigmatic guerrilla narrative, "manages to develop a unitary explanation that transcends individual sequences and episodes." This textual strategy would seem to be opposed to the postmodern attitude that resists totalizing projects. One need only recall the soul-wrenching execution-purges of weak or dissident comrades that frequently appear as cautionary tales in guerrilla narratives (in Guevara's 1967 *Pasajes de la guerra revolucionaria* [*Episodes of the Revolutionary War*] or Mario Payeras's 1980 *Los días de la selva* [*Days of the Jungle*], for example) to appreciate how far from the spirit of postmodernism this vein of testimonial writing diverges. Guevara's comment on the execution of a fellow revolutionary is chilling in this regard: "he served as an example, tragic it's true but valuable, so that the necessity of making our revolution a pure and not contaminated act might be understood."[22] This "intolerance for impurity" suggests that the substitution of one voice for another may merely replace one monologic discourse with another, and has no a priori claim to postmodernity.

There has been a curious re-creation of these guerrilla tactics in the current critical discourse on *testimonio.* In his insistence on the need for *testimonio* to break with literature as an institution or face charges of "modernist bias" or hegemonic postmodernity, Beverley echoes the absolutist "intolerance for impurities" that leads guerrilla fighters to purge their impure comrades. Yúdice's analysis of the *testimonio* also draws on a guerrilla-inspired rhetoric; his description of the genre as a "tactic by means of which people engage in the process of self-constitution and survival" strongly suggests a military strategy.[23]

Miguel Barnet is marginalized (purged) in both Beverley's and Yúdice's analyses of the *testimonio* as his testimonial novel is patently literary and thus does not conform to the prescriptive poetics they elaborate. Although Beverley is correct in discerning Barnet's "modernist bias in favor of textual collage and/or editorial elaboration in the preparation of a testimonial text," can any narrative claim to be the "direct, 'unliterary' narrative" that Beverley espouses?[24]

22. Juan Duchesne Winter, *La narrativa de testimonio en América Latina: cinco estudios,* 96, 113.

23. Yúdice, *"Testimonio* and Postmodernism," 18–19. The "tactics" used by subaltern classes to undermine their oppressors are also discussed in military terms by Certeau in *The Practice of Everyday Life.*

24. Beverley, *Against Literature,* 155.

Both Beverley and Yúdice make an exemplum of Rigoberta Menchú's *testimonio,* and yet it is undeniable that Elisabeth Burgos-Debray, Menchú's editor/transcriber, demonstrates "a modernist bias in favor of textual collage and/or editorial elaboration" evident in her juxtaposition of quotations from Asturias and the *Popol Vuh*—a mythic counterpoint that coincides with the high modernists' use of myth—and her admission that she gave the text the chronology of an autobiography, a traditional literary form in Western culture since at least the eighteenth century. At the same time, Beverley speaks of "testimonial expressionism" and other literary effects in Menchú's book, so even this exemplary 'non-literary' text comes dangerously close to enemy lines.[25] Any conceptualization of the *testimonio* that rejects Barnet for his 'literariness' would be hard-pressed not to condemn Burgos for her impurities as well.

What resonates in Beverley's attempt to distill the *testimonio* down to a kind of zero-degree, nonliterary, bare bones language devoid of tropes or rhetoric that must be read at a literal level is a notion of the Other's speech as minimal, uncluttered 'natural' language that ironically echoes Barnet's Romantic celebration of Montejo's speech as naturally poetic, "purer and more spontaneous . . . not tied to the mantle of rhetoric." In both versions the Other's voice is fetishized, either as primitive speech in the ethnological sense (Barnet) or as subaltern speech in the political sense (Beverley) as both are denied the coevalness with the literate Self that would allow for the process of transculturizing hybridity that marks the Latin American postmodern. Beverley's subaltern is fixed in a static epic pose of tragic conflict, while Barnet's is fixed in an eternally childlike state beyond historical time.

Meanwhile, Rigoberta Menchú's sojourn in Paris during her interview with Burgos-Debray finds her not blending in with the postmodern collage performed on urban streets in Paris since Carpentier's days as a *flâneur,* but confined to Burgos's kitchen—a space transformed into the site of eternal native purity and regress as Menchú performs her ethnicity in the baking of tortillas and the telling of native stories. If *I . . . Rigoberta Menchú* is a postmodern work, as some have claimed, it is only to the extent that Menchú's testimony manages to work against the grain of the "synthesizing allegory" of the ethnographic encounter between the modern Self and the time-locked indigenous Other played out in the Paris kitchen.[26]

25. Beverley, *Against Literature,* 81.
26. For a discussion of Menchú's strategies of resistance, see Sommer, "Rigoberta's Secrets."

A *testimonio* that more clearly partakes of the spirit of postmodernism might be Jesús Morales Bermúdez's *Memorial del tiempo* (Memorial of time, 1986). In her commentary on the novel, Cynthia Steele notes that Morales lived among the *choles* of northern Chiapas and years later wrote a testimonial novel marked by the use of the native dialect rather than standard Castilian, and the presence of several voices blending with the narrator's voice.[27] The novel's difficulty, due to its use of dialect, contrasts with the transparency called for in their different ways by Barnet and Beverley. Morales uses the dialect not to fetishize native speech as natural, but to draw attention to hybrid, oppositional, local resistance to incorporation in nationally constituted cultural forms.

The anthropological imagination in contemporary Latin American literature aligns itself with postmodernism when it rejects essentializing notions of the indigenous Other as pure origin or site of a sublime essence, when it focuses on marginalized or urban hybrid populations, when it renounces authorial, objectifying modes of knowledge and totalizing narratives or "synthesizing allegories," when it produces texts that are dialogic, polyvocal or collaborative in nature. The postmodern narrative of hybridity is, finally, "a story among other stories," as James Clifford would have it.[28] Nevertheless, such a story must be seen as "constructive" and "fruitful" in that it narrows the ontological divide between Self and Other, recasting the burden of Otherness as a liberating, empowering heterogeneity that reconfigures Latin America's historically problematic relation to modernity and its Others.

27. Cynthia Steele, "Indigenismo y posmodernidad: narrativa indigenista, *testimonio*, teatro campesino y video en el Chiapas finisecular."
28. Clifford and Marcus, eds., *Writing Culture,* 109.

# BIBLIOGRAPHY

Acosta-Belén, Edna, and Jean-Philippe Abraham. "Encuentro con Miguel Barnet." *Hispanófila* 104 (January 1992): 47–64.

Alonso, Carlos. "The Mourning After: García Márquez, Fuentes and the Meaning of Postmodernity in Spanish America." *MLN* 109 (1994): 252–67.

Andrade, Mário de. *Macunaíma*. Edited by Telê Porto Ancona Lopez. Brasília: Coleção Arquivos, 1988.

Aragon, Louis. *Le paysan de Paris*. Paris: Gallimard, 1953. Originally published in 1926.

———. *Nightwalker*. Translated by Frederick Brown. Englewood Cliffs, N.J.: Prentice-Hall, 1970.

Arguedas, José María. *Canciones y cuentos del pueblo quechua*. Lima: Ediciones Huascarán, 1949.

———. *Canto kechwa*. Ediciones Club del libro peruano, 1938.

———. *Formación de una cultura nacional indoamericana*. Edited by Angel Rama. 4th ed. México: Siglo XXI, 1987.

———. *Indios, mestizos y señores*. Lima: Editorial Horizonte, 1987.

———. *Los ríos profundos*. Madrid: Alianza Editorial, 1981. Originally published in 1958. *Deep Rivers*. Translated by Frances Horning Barraclough. Austin: University of Texas Press, 1978.

———. *Obras completas*. Vol. 1. Lima: Editorial Horizonte, 1983. Includes "El vengativo" (1934).

———. "¿Qué es el folklore?" *Cultura y pueblo* 1 (January–March 1964): 10–11.

———. *Relatos completos*. Edited by Jorge Lafforgue. Buenos Aires: Editorial Losada, 1977. Includes "El ayla" (1967), "Los escoleros" (1935), and "El horno viejo" (1967).

———. *Señores e indios: acerca de la cultura quechua*. Edited by Angel Rama. Buenos Aires: Calicanto Editorial, 1976.

————. *Todas las sangres*. Buenos Aires: Editorial Losada, 1973. Originally published in 1964.

————. *El zorro de arriba y el zorro de abajo*. Buenos Aires: Editorial Losada, 1971.

Arguedas, José María, and Francisco Izquierdo Ríos, eds. *Mitos, leyendas y cuentos peruanos*. 2d ed. Lima: Casa de la Cultura del Perú, 1970.

Asturias, Miguel Angel. *Hombres de maíz*. Madrid: Alianza Editorial, 1986. *Men of Maize*. Translated by Gerald Martin. Pittsburgh: University of Pittsburgh Press, 1993.

Avila, Francisco de. *Dioses y hombres de Huarochirí*. Translated and prologue by José María Arguedas. México: Siglo XXI, 1975. Originally published in 1966.

Barnet, Miguel. *Biografía de un cimarrón*. Madrid: Ediciones Alfaguara, 1984. Originally published in 1966. *Biography of a Runaway Slave*. Translated by W. Nick Hill. Willimantic, Conn.: Curbstone Press, 1994.

————. *La fuente viva*. Havana: Editorial Letras Cubanas, 1983.

————. "La novela testimonio: socio-literatura." In *La fuente viva,* 11–42.

————. "Testimonio y comunicación: una vía hacia la identidad." In *La fuente viva,* 43–60.

Barstow, Jean R. "Marriage between Human Beings and Animals: A Structuralist Discussion of Two Aymara Myths." *Anthropology* 5, no. 1 (May 1981): 71–88.

Barreda, Pedro. *The Black Protagonist in the Cuban Novel*. Translated by Page Bancroft. Amherst: University of Massachusetts Press, 1979.

Bastos, María Luisa. "Eficacias del verosímil no realista: dos novelas recientes de Juan José Saer." *La Torre: Revista de la Universidad de Puerto Rico* 4, no. 13 (January–March 1990): 1–20.

Basualdo, Ana. "El desierto retórico: Entrevista con Juan José Saer." *Quimera* 76 (1988): 12–15.

Bejel, Emilio. "Entrevista [with Miguel Barnet]." *Hispamérica* 29 (1981): 41–52.

Benítez-Rojo, Antonio. *The Repeating Island: The Caribbean and the Postmodern Perspective*. Translated by James E. Maraniss. Durham: Duke University Press, 1992.

Benvenuto, Bice, and Roger Kennedy. *The Works of Jacques Lacan: An Introduction*. London: Free Association Books, 1986.

Beverley, John. *Against Literature*. Minneapolis: University of Minnesota Press, 1993.

————. "The Margin at the Center: On *Testimonio* (Testimonial Narrative)." *Modern Fiction Studies* 35, no. 1 (spring 1989): 11–28.

Booker, M. Keith. *Vargas Llosa among the Postmodernists.* Gainesville: University Press of Florida, 1994.

Borges, Jorge Luis. "Story of the Warrior and the Captive." In *Labyrinths: Selected Stories and Other Writings,* edited by Donald A. Yates. Translated by James E. Irby. Norfolk, Conn.: New Directions Books, 1962, 127–31.

Bosi, Alfredo. "Situação de *Macunaíma.*" In *Macunaíma.* Edited by Telê Porto Ancona Lopez. Brasília: Coleção Arquivos, 1988: 171–81.

Brassaï. *The Secret Paris of the 30s.* Translated by Richard Miller. New York: Pantheon Books, 1976.

Bruner, Edward M. "Ethnography as Narrative." In *The Anthropology of Experience,* edited by E. Bruner and Victor Turner. Urbana: University of Illinois Press, 1986, 139–55.

Burgos-Debray, Elisabeth, ed. *Me llamo Rigoberta Menchú y así me nació la conciencia.* México: Siglo XXI, 1985. Originally published in 1983. *I . . . Rigoberta Menchú: An Indian Woman in Guatemala.* Translated by Ann Wright. London: Verso, 1984.

Butler, Christopher. *Early Modernism: Literature, Music, and Painting in Europe, 1900–1916.* Oxford: Clarendon Press, 1994.

Carpentier, Alejo. "Le 'Cante Jondo.'" *Bifur* 2 (1929): 69–84.

————. *¡Ecué-Yamba-O!* Madrid: Editorial España, 1933.

————. "Edgar Varèse escribe para el teatro." *Obras completas* 9: 273–77.

————. "Lettre des Antilles." *Bifur* 3 (1929): 91–105.

————. "La mécanisation de la musique." *Bifur* 5 (1930): 121–29.

————. "La musique cubaine." *Documents* 6 (1929): 324–27.

————. *La novela latinoamericana en vísperas de un nuevo siglo.* México: Siglo XXI, 1981. Includes "America ante la joven literatura europea."

————. *Obras completas.* Vols. 1, 8–9. México: Siglo XXI, 1986.

————. *Los pasos perdidos.* Edited by Roberto González Echevarría. Madrid: Cátedra, 1985. Originally published in 1953. *The Lost Steps.* Translated by Harriet de Onís. New York: Knopf, 1956.

Carr, Helen. "Woman/Indian: 'The American' and His Others." In *Proceedings of the Essex Conference on the Sociology of Literature: Europe and Its Others,* vol. 2, edited by Francis Barker et al. Colchester: University of Essex, 1985, 46–60.

Castro, Carlo Antonio. *Siluetas mexicanas*. México: Editorial Amate, 1980.

Castro Klarén, Sara. "Crimen y castigo: sexualidad en José María Arguedas." *Revista Iberoamericana* 49, no. 122 (January–March 1985): 55–65.

———. "José María Arguedas, Testimonio sobre preguntas de Sara Castro Klarén." *Hispamérica* 4, no. 10 (1975): 45–54.

Certeau, Michel de. *The Practice of Everyday Life*. Translated by Steven Rendall. Berkeley: University of California Press, 1984.

———. *The Writing of History*. Translated by Tom Conley. New York: Columbia University Press, 1988.

Challaye, Félicien. "Souvenirs sur la colonisation." *Bifur* 8 (1931).

Chanady, Amaryll. "Saer's Fictional Representation of the Amerindian in the Context of Modern Historiography." In *Amerindian Images and the Legacy of Columbus*, edited by René Jara and Nicholas Spadaccini. *Hispanic Issues* 9. Minneapolis: University of Minnesota Press, 1992, 678–708.

Chapman, Anne. *El fin de un mundo: los Selk'nam de Tierra del Fuego*. Buenos Aires: Vázquez Mazzini Editores, 1989.

Clifford, James. "Negrophilia." In *A New History of French Literature*, edited by Denis Hollier. Cambridge: Harvard University Press, 1989, 901–8.

———. *The Predicament of Culture: Twentieth-Century Ethnography, Literature, and Arts*. Cambridge: Harvard University Press, 1988.

Clifford, James, and George E. Marcus, eds. *Writing Culture: The Poetics and Politics of Ethnography*. Berkeley: University of California Press, 1986.

Colás, Santiago. *Postmodernity in Latin America: The Argentine Paradigm*. Durham: Duke University Press, 1994.

Corbatta, Jorgelina. "Juan José Saer: Narración versus realidad." *RLA: Romance Languages Annual* 3 (1991): 391–96.

Cornejo Polar, Antonio. "Las figuraciones transculturales en la obra de Augusto Roa Bastos." *Hispamérica* 20, no. 59 (August 1991): 3–10.

———. "El sentido de la narrativa de Arguedas." In *Recopilación de textos sobre José María Arguedas*, edited by Juan Larco. Havana: Casa de las Américas, 1976, 45–72.

———. *Los universos narrativos de José María Arguedas*. Buenos Aires: Editorial Losada, 1973.

Cortázar, Julio. *Rayuela*. Edited by Andrés Amorós. Madrid: Cátedra, 1989.

Originally published in 1963. *Hopscotch.* Translated by Gregory Rabassa. New York: Pantheon, 1966.

Crapanzano, Vincent. "Hermes' Dilemma: The Masking of Subversion in Ethnographic Description." In *Writing Culture: The Poetics and Politics of Ethnography,* edited by Clifford James and George Marcus, 51–76.

———. *Tuhami: Portrait of a Moroccan.* Chicago: University of Chicago Press, 1989.

DaMatta, Roberto. *Carnivals, Rogues, and Heroes: An Interpretation of the Brazilian Dilemma.* Translated by John Drury. Notre Dame: University of Notre Dame Press, 1991.

Douglas, Mary. *Purity and Danger: An Analysis of Concepts of Pollution and Taboo.* London: Routledge and Kegan Paul, 1966.

Duchesne Winter, Juan. "Etnopoética y estrategias discursivas en *Canto de sirena.*" *Revista de crítica literaria latinoamericana* 20 (1984): 189–205.

———. *La narrativa de testimonio en América Latina: cinco estudios.* Río Piedras: Universidad de Puerto Rico, 1992.

Fabian, Johannes. *Time and the Other: How Anthropology Makes Its Object.* New York: Columbia University Press, 1983.

Fischer, Michael M. J. "Autobiographical Voices (1, 2, 3) and Mosaic Memory: Experimental Sondages in the (Post)modern World." In *Autobiography and Postmodernism,* edited by Kathleen Ashley, Leigh Gilmore, and Gerald Peters. Amherst: University of Massachusetts Press, 1994, 79–129.

———. "Ethnicity and the Postmodern Arts of Memory." In *Writing Culture: The Poetics and Politics of Ethnography,* edited by Clifford James and George Marcus, 194–233.

Flores, Juan. "Cortijo's Revenge: New Mappings of Puerto Rican Culture." In *On Edge: The Crisis of Contemporary Latin American Culture,* edited by George Yúdice, Jean Franco, and Juan Flores. Minneapolis: University of Minnesota Press, 187–205.

Forgues, Roland. *Del pensamiento dialéctico al pensamiento trágico.* Translated by Claude Allaigre. Lima: Editorial Horizonte, 1984.

Foster, Hal. " 'Primitive' Scenes." *Critical Inquiry* 20 (autumn 1993): 69–102.

———. *Recodings: art, spectacle, cultural politics.* Port Townsend, Wash.: Bay Press, 1985.

Franco, Jean. "The Nation as Imagined Community." In *The New Histori-cism,* edited by H. Aram Veeser. New York and London: Routledge, 1989, 204–12.

———. "Pastiche in Contemporary Latin American Literature." *Studies in Contemporary Literature* 14, no. 1 (winter 1990): 95–107.

———. *Plotting Women: Gender and Representation in Mexico.* New York: Columbia University Press, 1989.

Galeano, Eduardo. *Memoria del fuego: los nacimientos.* México: Siglo XXI, 1982.

Gallegos, Rómulo. *Canaíma.* Buenos Aires: Espasa-Calpe, 1965. Originally published in 1941.

García Canclini, Néstor. *Culturas híbridas: Estrategias para entrar y salir de la modernidad.* México: Editorial Grijalbo, 1990.

———. "Los estudios culturales de los 80 a los 90: perspectivas antropoló-gicas y sociológicas en América Latina." In *Postmodernidad en la periferia: enfoques latinoamericanos de la nueva teoría cultural,* edited by Hermann Herlinghaus and Monika Walter. Berlin: Langer Verlag, 1994, 111–33.

Gilman, Sander. *Difference and Pathology: Stereotypes of Sexuality, Race, and Madness.* Ithaca: Cornell University Press, 1985.

Golte, Jürgen. "Latin America: The Anthropology of Conquest." In *Anthro-pology: Ancestors and Heirs,* edited by Stanley Diamond. The Hague: Mouton, 1980, 377–93.

González Echevarría, Roberto. *Alejo Carpentier: The Pilgrim at Home.* Ithaca: Cornell University Press, 1977.

———. *Myth and Archive: A Theory of Latin American Narrative.* Cam-bridge: Cambridge University Press, 1990.

———. *The Voice of the Masters: Writing and Authority in Modern Latin American Literature.* Austin: University of Texas Press, 1985.

Gnutzmann, Rita. *"El entenado* o la respuesta de Saer a las crónicas." *Iris* (1992): 23–36.

Greenblatt, Stephen. "Learning to Curse: Aspects of Linguistic Colonialism in the Sixteenth Century." In *First Images of America: The Impact of the New World on the Old,* edited by Fredi Chiapelli. Berkeley: University of California Press, 1976, 561–80.

———. *Marvelous Possessions: The Wonder of the New World.* Chicago: University of Chicago Press, 1991.

Guiteras Holmes, Calixta. *Perils of the Soul: The World View of a Tzotzil Indian*. New York: Free Press of Glencoe, 1961.

Harrison, Regina. *Signs, Songs, and Memory in the Andes*. Austin: University of Texas Press, 1989.

Herbert, Christopher. *Culture and Anomie: Ethnographic Imagination in the Nineteenth Century*. Chicago: Chicago University Press, 1991.

Hollier, Denis, ed. *The College of Sociology 1937–1939*. Translated by Betsy Wing. Minneapolis: University of Minnesota Press, 1988.

Hudson, William Henry. *Green Mansions*. New York: Dover, 1989. Originally published in 1904.

Hutcheon, Linda. *A Theory of Parody: The Teachings of Twentieth-Century Art Forms*. New York: Methuen, 1985.

Ibarra, Jorge. "La herencia científica de Fernando Ortiz." *Revista Iberoamericana* 56, nos. 152–153: 1339–51.

Im Thurn, Everard F. *Among the Indians of Guiana*. New York: Dover, 1967. Originally published in 1883.

Kerr, Lucille. "Gestures of Authorship: Lying to Tell the Truth in Elena Poniatowska's *Hasta no verte Jesús mío*." In *Reclaiming the Author: Figures and Fictions from Spanish America*. Durham: Duke University Press, 1992, 46–64.

Kilgour, Maggie. *From Communion to Cannibalism: An Anatomy of Metaphors of Incorporation*. Princeton: Princeton University Press, 1990.

Kirsner, Douglas. "Sartre and the Collective Neurosis of Our Time." *Yale French Studies* 68 (1985): 206–25.

Klengel, Susane. "*Maíra* de Darcy Ribeiro: la búsqueda de lo auténtico." In *Homenaje a Alejandro Losada,* edited by José Morales Saravia. Lima: Latinoamericana Editores, 1986, 207–20.

Kroeber, Theodora. *Ishi in Two Worlds: A Biography of the Last Wild Indian in North America*. Berkeley: University of California Press, 1976. Originally published in 1961.

Langness, L. L., and Gelya Frank. *Lives: An Anthropological Approach to Biography*. Novato, Calif.: Chandler and Sharp, 1981.

Larsen, Neil. *Modernism and Hegemony: A Materialist Critique of Aesthetic Agencies*. Minneapolis: University of Minnesota Press, 1990.

Lechner, Norbert. "A Disenchantment Called Postmodernism." *Boundary 2* 20, no. 3 (fall 1993): 122–39.

Léry, Jean de. *History of a Voyage to the Land of Brasil*. Translated by Janet Whatley. Berkeley: University of California Press, 1990.

Letvin, Alice. *Sacrifice in the Surrealist Novel: The Impact of Early Theories of Primitive Religion on the Depiction of Violence in Modern Fiction.* New York: Garland, 1990.

Lévi-Strauss, Claude. *Tristes Tropiques.* Translated by John and Doreen Weightman. New York: Washington Square Press, 1973.

Lienhard, Martin. *La voz y su huella: escritura y conflicto étnico-social en América Latina.* Hanover: Ediciones del Norte, 1991.

Lispector, Clarice. *Laços de família.* 11th ed. Rio de Janeiro: Livraria José Olympio Editora, 1979. *Family Ties.* Translated by Giovanni Pontiero. Austin: University of Texas Press, 1972.

López de Gómara, Francisco. *Historia general de las Indias.* Vols. 1–2. Madrid: España-Calpe, 1932. Originally printed in 1552.

Losfield, Eric, ed. *Tracts surréalistes et déclarations collectives.* Paris: Terrain vague, avec le concours du Centre Nationale de la Recherche Scientifique, 1980.

Luis, William. "The Politics of Memory and Miguel Barnet's *The Autobiography of a Runaway Slave.*" *MLN* 104, no. 2 (1989): 475–91.

MacCormack, Sabine. *Religion in the Andes: Vision and Imagination in Early Colonial Peru.* Princeton: Princeton University Press, 1991.

Manganaro, Marc, ed. *Modernist Anthropology: From Fieldwork to Text.* Princeton: Princeton University Press, 1990.

Manns, Patricio. *Actas del Alto Bío Bío.* Madrid: Ediciones Michay, 1985.

Martínez, Gregorio. *Canto de sirena.* Lima: Mosca Azul Editores, 1977.

Marzal, Manuel M. *Historia de la antropología indigenista: México y Perú.* Lima: Fondo Editorial, 1981.

Mignolo, Walter D. "When Speaking Was Not Good Enough: Illiterates, Barbarians, Savages, and Cannibals." In *Amerindian Images and the Legacy of Columbus.* Edited by René Jara and Nicholas Spadaccini. Minneapolis: University of Minnesota Press, 1992, 312–45.

Miller, Christopher. *Blank Darkness: Africanist Discourse in French.* Chicago: University of Chicago Press, 1985.

Montaigne, Michel de. "On cannibals." In *Essays,* translated by J. M. Cohen. Middlesex: Penguin, 1958: 105–19. Originally composed 1579–1580.

Motolinía, Fray Toribio de. *Historia de la Nueva España.* Edited by Georges Baudot. Madrid: Clásicos Castalia, 1985.

Muñoz, Silverio. *José María Arguedas y el mito de la salvación por la cultura.* Minneapolis: Instituto para el Estudio de Ideologías y Literatura, 1980.

Ortega, Julio. "Texto, comunicación y cultura en *Los ríos profundos* de José María Arguedas." *Nueva Revista de Filología Hispánica* 31: 44–82.

Ortiz, Fernando. *Hampa afro-cubana: los negros brujos.* Miami: Ediciones Universal, 1973. Originally published in 1906.

Pagden, Anthony. *The Fall of Natural Man: The American Indian and the Origins of Comparative Ethnology.* Cambridge: Cambridge University Press, 1982.

Pané, Fray Ramón. *Relación acerca de las antigüedades de los indios.* Edited by José Juan Arrom. México: Siglo XXI, 1974.

Paz, Octavio. *Lévi-Strauss o el nuevo festín de Esopo.* Barcelona: Editorial Seix Barral, 1993. Originally published in 1967.

Piedra, José. "The Afro-Cuban Esthetics of Alejo Carpentier." Ph.D. diss., Yale University, 1985.

Plato. *The Symposium.* Translated by Walter Hamilton. London: Penguin, 1951.

Pozas, Ricardo. *Juan Pérez Jolote: Biografía de un tzotzil.* 9th ed. México: Fondo de Cultura Económica, 1980.

Prada Oropeza, Renato. "De lo testimonial al testimonio: Notas para un deslinde del discurso-testimonio." In *Testimonio y literatura,* edited by René Jara and Hernán Vidal. Minneapolis: Institute for the Study of Ideologies and Literature, 1986.

Pratt, Mary Louise. "Conventions of Representation: Where Discourse and Ideology Meet." In *Contemporary Perceptions of Language: Interdisciplinary Dimensions,* edited by Heidi Byrnes. Washington, D.C.: Georgetown University Press, 1982, 139–55.

———. "Fieldwork in Common Places." In *Writing Culture: The Poetics and Politics of Ethnography,* edited by James Clifford and George E. Marcus, 27–50.

*Primer encuentro de narradores peruanos.* Lima: Casa de la Cultura, 1969.

Rabinow, Paul. "Representations Are Social Facts: Modernity and Post-Modernity in Anthropology." In *Writing Culture: The Poetics and Politics of Ethnography,* edited by James Clifford and George E. Marcus, 234–61.

Rama, Angel. *Transculturación narrativa en América Latina.* México: Siglo XXI, 1982.

Ramos, Julio. *Desencuentros de la modernidad en América Latina:*

*Literatura y política en el siglo XIX*. México: Fondo de Cultura Económica, 1989.

Rawson, C. J. "Cannibalism and Fiction: Reflections on Narrative Form and 'Extreme' Situations." *Genre* 10, no. 4 (winter 1977): 667–711.

Redfield, Robert. "The Primitive World View." In *Human Nature and the Study of Society: From the Papers of Robert Redfield,* edited by Margaret Park Redfield. Vol. 1. Chicago: University of Chicago Press, 1962, 269–82.

Ribeiro, Darcy. *Fronteras indígenas de la civilización*. Translated by Julio Rossiello. México: Siglo XXI, 1971.

———. *Kadiwéu: Ensaios etnológicos sobre o saber, o azar e a beleza*. Rio de Janeiro: Petrópolis, 1980.

———. *Maíra: romance*. Rio de Janeiro: Civilização Brasileira, 1981. *Maíra*. Translated by E. H. Goodland and Thomas Colchie. New York: Random House, 1984.

———. *Sobre o obvio*. Rio de Janeiro: Editora Guanabara, 1986.

———. *Testemunho*. São Paulo: Siciliano, 1990.

Richard, Nelly. "Latinoamérica y la posmodernidad." In *Postmodernidad en la periferia: enfoques latinoamericanos de la nueva teoría cultural,* edited by Hermann Herlinghaus and Monika Walter. Berlin: Langer Verlag, 1994, 210–22.

Richman, Michele. *Reading Georges Bataille: Beyond the Gift*. Baltimore: Johns Hopkins University Press, 1982.

Rigdon, Susan M. *The Culture Facade: Art, Science, and Politics in the Work of Oscar Lewis*. Urbana and Chicago: University of Illinois Press, 1988.

Rincón, Carlos. "Nociones surrealistas, concepción del lenguaje y función ideológico-literaria del realismo mágico en Miguel Angel Asturias." *Escritura* 3, nos. 5–6 (1978): 25–61.

Rivera, José Eustasio. *La vorágine*. Santiago: Empresa Letras, 1933. Originally published in 1924.

Rivière, Georges Henri. "Le Musée d'Ethnographie du Trocadéro." *Documents* 1 (1929).

Rodríguez Juliá, Edgardo. *El entierro de Cortijo*. Río Piedras: Ediciones Huracán, 1983.

Romero de Valle, Emilia. "Juegos infantiles tradicionales en el Perú." *25 Estudios de Folklore*. México: Universidad Nacional Autónoma de México Instituto de Investigaciones Estéticas, 1971, 329–31.

Rosa, Nicolás. "La crítica literaria contemporánea." In *Historia de la literatura argentina.* Vol. 5. Buenos Aires: Centro Editor de América Latina, 1982, 385–408.

Rosaldo, Renato. *Culture and Truth: The Remaking of Social Analysis.* Boston: Beacon Press, 1989.

Rowe, William. "Arguedas: música, conocimiento y transformación social." *Revista de crítica literaria latinoamericana* 13, no. 25 (1987): 97–107.

———. *Mito e ideología en la obra de José María Arguedas.* Lima: Instituto Nacional de Cultura, 1979.

Rowe, William, and Vivian Schelling. *Memory and Modernity: Popular Culture in Latin America.* London: Verso, 1991.

Saer, Juan José. *El entenado.* México: Folios Ediciones, 1983. *The Witness.* Translated by Margaret Jull Costa. London: Serpents Tail, 1990.

Said, Edward. *Culture and Imperialism.* New York: Knopf, 1993.

———. *Orientalism.* New York: Vintage, 1979.

———. "Representing the Colonized: Anthropology's Interlocutors." *Critical Inquiry* 15 (winter 1989): 205–25.

Sánchez, Matilde. "Saer: 'La literatura es objeto y misterio.'" *Tiempo Argentino,* February 10, 1985.

Sangari, Kumkum. "The Politics of the Possible." *Cultural Critique* 7 (1987): 157–86.

Santiago, Silviano. "A trajetória de um livro." In *Macunaíma.* Edited by Telê Porto Ancona Lopez. Brasília: Coleção Arquivos, 1988, 182–93.

Sarup, Madan. *An Introductory Guide to Post-Structuralism and Postmodernism.* 2d ed. Athens: University of Georgia Press, 1993.

———. *Jacques Lacan.* Toronto: University of Toronto Press, 1992.

Schaeffner, André. "Des Instruments de Musique dans un Musée d'Ethnographie." *Documents* 5 (1929).

Schneider, Luis Mario. *México y el surrealismo (1925–1950).* México: Arte y Libros, 1978.

Sklodowska, Elzbieta. *"Biografía de un cimarrón* de Miguel Barnet: revisión de la historia afrocubana." *Historiografía y Bibliografía Americanistas* 37 (1983): 43–59.

Sommer, Doris. "Rigoberta's Secrets." *Latin American Perspectives* 70 (summer 1991): 32–50.

Sontag, Susan. "The Anthropologist as Hero." In *Claude Lévi-Strauss: The*

*Anthropologist as Hero,* edited by E. Nelson and Tanya Hayes. Cambridge, Mass.: M.I.T. Press, 1970, 184–96.

Spencer, Frank. "Some Notes on the Attempt to Apply Photography to Anthropometry during the Second Half of the Nineteeth Century." In *Anthropology & Photography 1860–1920,* edited by Elizabeth Edwards. New Haven: Yale University Press, 1992.

Stallybrass, Peter, and Allon White. *The Politics and Poetics of Transgression.* Ithaca: Cornell University Press, 1986.

Steele, Cynthia. "Indigenismo y posmodernidad: narrativa indigenista, *testimonio,* teatro campesino y video en el Chiapas finisecular." *Revista de crítica literaria latinoamericana* 19, no. 38 (1993): 249–60.

Stocking, George. "Introduction: The Basic Assumptions of Boasian Anthropology." In *A Franz Boas Reader: The Shaping of American Anthropology,* edited by George Stocking. Chicago: University of Chicago Press, 1974. Midway Reprint, 1989, 1–20.

Street, Brian. "British Popular Anthropology: Exhibiting and Photographing the Other." In *Anthropology & Photography 1860–1920,* edited by Elizabeth Edwards. New Haven: Yale University Press, 1992.

Taussig, Michael. *Mimesis and Alterity: A Particular History of the Senses.* New York and London: Routledge, 1993.

———. *Shamanism, Colonialism, and the Wild Man: A Study in Terror and Healing.* Chicago: University of Chicago Press, 1987.

Tedlock, Dennis. *The Spoken Word and the Work of Interpretation.* Philadelphia: University of Pennsylvania Press, 1983.

Tello, Julio C. *Páginas Escogidas.* Edited by Toribio Mejía Xesspe. Lima: Universidad Nacional Mayor de San Marcos, 1967.

Todorov, Tzvetan. *The Conquest of America: The Question of the Other.* Translated by Richard Howard. New York: Harper and Row, 1985.

Torgovnick, Marianna. *Gone Primitive: Savage Intellects, Modern Lives.* Chicago: University of Chicago Press, 1990.

Tyler, Stephen A. "Ethnography, Intertextuality, and the End of Description." *American Journal of Semiotics* 3, no. 4 (1985): 83–98.

———. "Postmodern Ethnography: From Document of the Occult to Occult Document." In *Writing Culture: The Poetics and Politics of Ethnography,* edited by Clifford James and George Marcus, 122–40.

Vargas Llosa, Mario. *El hablador.* Barcelona: Seix Barral, 1987. *The Storyteller.* Translated by Helen Lane. New York: Farrar Straus Giroux, 1989.

———. *José María Arguedas: entre sapos y halcones*. Madrid: Ediciones Cultura Hispánica, 1978.

Vázquez, Carmen. "El mundo maravilloso de Alejo Carpentier." *Revista de Estudios Hispánicos* 10 (1983): 17–27.

Ventura, Roberto. "Literature, Anthropology, and Popular Culture in Brazil: From José de Alencar to Darcy Ribeiro." *Komparatistische Hefte* 2 (1985): 35–47.

Vera-León, Antonio. "Montejo, Barnet, el cimarronaje y la escritura de la historia." *Inti* 29–30 (1989): 3–16.

Vidal, Luis Fernando. "Review of *Canto de sirena*." *Revista de crítica literaria latinoamericana* 6 (1977).

Webster, Steven. "Postmodernist Theory and the Sublimation of Maori Culture." *Oceania* 63, no. 3 (March 1993): 222–39.

Young, Robert J. C. *Colonial Desire: Hybridity in Theory, Culture and Race*. London and New York: Routledge, 1995.

———. *White Mythologies: Writing History and the West*. London and New York: Routledge, 1990.

Yúdice, George. "El conflicto de posmodernidades." *Nuevo Texto Crítico* 7 (1991): 19–33.

———. *"Testimonio* and Postmodernism." *Latin American Perspectives* 70 (summer 1991): 15–31.

# Index

**153**